OWNING Patricia

A STORY OF BREAKING FREE

Owen Valley High School
Library
622 W. St. Hwy 46
Spencer, IN 47460

OWNING
Patricia
A STORY OF BREAKING FREE

PATRICIA BONELLI

Book Publishers Network

Book Publishers Network
P. O. Box 2256
Bothell, WA 98041
425 483-3040
www.bookpublishersnetwork.com

Copyright 2011 by Patricia Bonelli

Formerly titled
Where Do We Go From Here:
A Story of Courage, Redemption and Truth

All rights reserved. No part of this publication may be translated, reproduced, or transmitted in
any form or by any means, in whole or in part, electronic, or mechanical including photocopying, recording, or by any information storage or retrieval system withouth prior permission in writing from the publisher.

Publisher and editor are not liable for any typographical errors, content mistakes, inaccuracies, or omissions related to the information in this book.

Product trade names or trademarks mentioned throughout this publication remain property of their respective owners.

10 9 8 7 6 5 4 3 2 1

LCCN 2009928996
ISBN 10 1-935359-64-9
ISBN 13 978-1-935359-64-7

Cover design: Kris Harmon, Reflection Studios
Text design: Kris Harmon, Reflection Studios

Photography by brubakerphotography.com

Dedication

For the teachers I have loved along the way ~ and the god in me that never gives up.

When a fly ball hits you in the head grab some ice
but don't stop participating in the game.

TABLE OF CONTENTS

INTRODUCTION Full Disclosure 1

CHAPTER 1 Write Your Life, He Said 3
*A relationship with your whole self is necessary to show
up whole in the world.*

CHAPTER 2 First Dumping Ground 11
Quiet anger that implodes is as destructive as rage that explodes.

CHAPTER 3 Far Beyond Control 21
*Understand your motives before you act. If you are guided by
fear, selfishness, or retaliation—stop.*

CHAPTER 4 Working Hard for the Money 33
*We all have an Achilles' heel that shows us where we are
limited and need the most work.*

CHAPTER 5 Climbing Up While Going Down 51
*Set your bar high, but retain your flexibility so you can move
it when necessary to accomplish your end goal.*

CHAPTER 6 A Witness to Change 67
Every place I find myself is the result of my own decisions.

CHAPTER 7 It's Not Just Me Anymore 77
Relationships are required if you want to thrive.

CHAPTER 8 She Did Love Me, After All 87
*Needing love and approval from others is wasted energy.
Others come and go, but your self is always with you.*

CHAPTER 9 How About A Receptionist? 95
*When in doubt, look in the mirror and say: I believe in you.
Do this over and over again. Change will manifest.*

CHAPTER 10 **Irony is Alive and Well** 103
*As you cross the bridge to accomplishment, tenacity
strengthens belief in your goal.*

CHAPTER 11 **Real Sexual Liberation** 113
Liberation is the freedom to be your dreams.

CHAPTER 12 **The Past Returns** 127
To be honest in the face of conflict is true nobility.

CHAPTER 13 **Stubbornly Making a Difference—or Not** 139
*Once you are comfortable with your own pain, you
can become comfortable with the pain of others.*

CHAPTER 14 **Everyone Wants a Piece of Me** 155
*Broken dreams are new opportunities to create triumph
by setting new intentions.*

CHAPTER 15 **Let's Make a Deal** 167
Nothing replaces human touch.

CHAPTER 16 **Going Within** 173
*Listen to your gut even if it leads you somewhere you
don't want to go.*

CHAPTER 17 **The Spirit of Aloha** 181
*Share love with strangers as well as those you consider safe.
With No expectation of return, love flows without effort.*

CHAPTER 18 **Dreams That Come True Have Their Own Destiny**... 191
*If someone betrays or disappoints you, forgive them. They may
have done the best they could under the circumstances—you
don't have to like it but you must let it go.*

CHAPTER 19 **Go Back and Learn It Again** 201
*Courage through faith will get you where you need to be
every time-even when you want to be elsewhere.*

CHAPTER 20 **Aloha, Dear Reader…And The Beat Goes On** 215
Love is the ability to extend yourself for the well-being of another.

Acknowledgments

Gina for your encouragement to write my truth.

All my children for their personal strength
and the gift of believing in possibilities.

Ashley for her vote of confidence and technical assistance.

The endorsement and kind words from my ex-husband, Clark.

Kim Pearson for staying committed and on board
throughout the duration.

Nancy Cleary, at Wyatt-McKenzie for your professional integrity.

I want to extend a heartfelt thank you for those who
have so kindly encouraged me along this journey.

Kelly Caldwell, Chuck and Kathy, Jill Daniel, Susan Kincaid,
Sylvia Brown and the Marshall Family

Special thanks to my lifelong friend Nancy of 40 years with
whom I still share a committed loving sisterhood.

Graphic design by Kris Harmon at Reflection Studios.
www.reflectionstudiosonline.com

ENDORSEMENT FOR AFFINITY PLACE

This book is a platform from which greater good and accomplishment is to be derived. As we accept our gifts with gratitude we widen the scope of compassion and thus our aptitude expands beyond self. It is here we may be of service to others in such a way that we truly pay forward the sum of our experiences. The success of this book will support the implementation of the Affinity Place program. This non-profit program has been developed under the Agape Foundation for Women Inc. The program is designed to serve young women aged 17-21, providing them with a strong skill set and the internal discipline and confidence to become powerful leaders and productive members within their communities.

Our Mission Statement
The Affinity center is a resource-based learning program for young women of California. Our goal is to mentor participants while they acquire skills to live powerfully and productively as they create their own independence. Our purpose is to strengthen families, grow sustainable personal development, cultivate leadership, and foster respect for all. Our supportive environment combined with proficient professionals, an intense curriculum, program tools and lifestyle skills is designed to yield advanced results. Affinity Place is committed to building a solid foundation for women to become effective contributing members of society.

AFFINITY...WHERE ENERGY IS CONNECTED INTO THE LIGHT
Affinity—Marked by community of interest with compassion: KINSHIP: an attraction to or liking for something.

We are always where we are supposed to be. The lesson is in acceptance of what has occurred while remaining open to the experiences in our path.

"This book illuminates the legal and economic problems of girls and women searching for freedom and equality. Patricia is a perfect example of a woman who turned the table son the system. It's life stories like this that can turn things around by illuminating the truth."

—Margo St. James

COURAGE:

The ability to meet one's perception of danger
without being held back by fear

REDEMPTION:

To give back possession of;
to turn away from inadequacy and failure

TRUTH:

To be in accurate agreement with the facts

INTRODUCTION

FULL DISCLOSURE

Everyone's life conveys a story. In our public conversations and even in our own minds, we often prefer the edited, cleaned-up versions. We carefully omit the scenes of darkness and ugly thoughts from our history. We strive for a non-threatening image so we can, on the surface, look and be whole to ourselves and the outside world.

I've had decades of practice in hiding behind an edited life, a half truth. Painful events caused me to devalue who I had been. Voices echoed: "People leave you," and you are not worthy." I did not ever want that to be my story, then or now…but that's how my life got started, with abandonment, followed by neglect, escalated to exploitation.

When my adoptive parents repeatedly reminded me as a child, "We didn't have to have you," my young heart broke as I longed for someone to tell me and show me, what unconditional love was.

Uncomfortable events happen to everyone. I believe it was my dedication to improve the quality of my own life, which finally gave me the strength then allowed me to break free from once limiting constraints—and now owning my unedited truth.

I wanted to write about what is real: that stuff we sweep under the carpet, hide in the closet, or file away to deal with "later." I wanted to write about believing in the good and achieving the best, even when the journey is through the darkness. In this book I have shared my experiences and the process of becoming empowered as a result of remaining open. I invite you to jump in and do your own excavation.

Following each chapter is my personal reflection, and an opportunity and invitation for you to answer the questions posed and join the journey too.

My journey began with seeking the advice of a writing coach, someone who I thought could guide me through writing the edited version of my story, the version I was willing to share with an audience on my terms. Well, that did not go exactly the way I had planned. What I did not realize at that time was in order to help others and encourage people to understand what I had learned—they had to first hear my story.

Sometimes we need to relate our stories to one another to share the tragedies we have faced in life. We gain comfort in knowing we are not alone. By telling the unedited version of my story this would allow me to reach out to others who have struggled or have felt lost or abandoned at some point in their own life no matter what the of the details of their story may have been.

I hope by reading this book and experiencing the events including my fight for survival, you will feel inspired, confident, valued, safe and capable of anything and everything you believe you deserve. Life really is what you make of it, and each of us has the power to correct and change it.

CHAPTER ONE

WRITE YOUR LIFE, HE SAID

A relationship with your whole self is necessary to show up whole in the world

He was an idiot. And I was disgusted!

Why was I here, paying this weird-looking man to give me advice I knew was wrong?

His name was Conrad, and I hired him to be my writing coach because I wanted to write a book, even though I never considered myself a writer. I had lived a "hard life," as they say, and through it I had learned some valuable lessons. I thought if I could share those lessons with other people, they, too, would get some value out of them. Maybe it would make sense of some of the pain I had endured and provide some type of redemption.

But I wanted to share the lessons. Conrad wanted me to share the actual events. "You have to write your life," he said.

What a crock.

First of all, don't tell me I have to do anything. It's the surest way to make me run a mile in the opposite direction. I know all about have to. Like they say—been there, done that.

But mostly, I didn't want to share the events of my life. The pain I'd been through, the bad choices I made—why would I want to revisit them? Why go back down into the depths that took me so long, and took so much work, to climb out of?

By the age of 12, I found myself left to my own devices as to how I would provide for myself with no sense of who I was. I chose a series of degrading and desperate corridors to walk through: from an out-of-control runaway living on the streets as a middle-school dropout, to being exploited by a pimp, and becoming the domestic partner of a drug runner; a single mother of three children by the age of 23. The road from hell had my name engraved in the cement poured during my youth. When I finally got my life together, I had only a seventh-grade education, and the only way I knew how to make money was on my back.

In an ironic twist, no one would believe if it were fiction, I managed to get a college education plus an MBA degree, and I achieved a successful career as, of all things, a law enforcement officer. For nearly twenty years I was a parole/probation officer working with people whose choices, like mine before them, had led them into desperate places.

I know a lot of stories, my own and others'. They are full of humiliating acts and ugly thoughts perpetuated by betrayal, loneliness, ignorance and despair.

And Conrad thought that I should write these stories down! To do that, to relive those memories, I'd have to jump back into the gutter. For God's sake, I busted my ass to get out. Why would I want to do that to myself? Or my kids—what kind of legacy would I be leaving them? They knew little about my early life, and I wanted to keep it that way. And what about my future relationships with men? I'm sort of an expert on how men view women. I had no confidence that any man would ever understand what I had been through, or why.

Besides, who would care? Why would readers want to fill their minds with remnants of my garbage? I didn't see how that could help anyone. How could these dark stories light the way toward living a good and purpose-filled life, the kind of life I'd worked so hard to build?

When I first showed Conrad my writing, he didn't seem impressed. "There's no story here," he said. "You're telling me what you think now. I want to know what you did then."

I argued with him. I shared some of my experiences, to show him how totally unsuited they were for a book about creating a good life. I told him there was no way I was going to write a book about my past. No way would I share stuff like being raped, being beaten, being treated like something you throw away. That was over; no one beat me anymore. I had journaled, meditated and studied with spiritual teachers. My soul had been healed. I was passionate about sharing my way through the darkness and the destination of my journey which was love and forgiveness. This is what I wanted to share with others. Light through love, not darkness.

Conrad listened and nodded, but said little as I ranted at him. Mostly he just looked at me. When I stopped, he said, "You're not getting it. The raw stuff of life is beautiful."

I didn't actually hear his words, probably because I was too twisted to listen. In essence he told me that my true success in writing would only come about by writing from the core of my life experiences. They were the source of my authentic writing and they were the truth. He even said the reason I had these experiences was so that I could write about them. They were my writing credentials. I had lived them in order to share them.

This would be my greatest challenge. I was inspired to give back, but I didn't think I'd have to go back to the trenches for one more round. I didn't think that to share the present I'd have to visit the past. That is when the value of coming full circle hit me between the eyes and a voice beyond said, "You're good to go."

After a few weeks passed, the audacity of Conrad's recommendation settled in. I decided to listen to the tape of the session we had together. This time, I could really hear Conrad's words. I opened myself, mind body and soul to the wisdom in his prescription. I contemplated the pros and cons then got on my knees and asked for guidance. I listened to the tape again and I erased my reaction to his suggestion. I let his recommendation stand on its own without my concerns for myself at the forefront. And I finally got it.

It's always about ego, isn't it? I had a picture in my mind of what I thought my book should be. I thought it should be about telling the reader how I wanted others to have a good life. I wanted to share how I came through challenging episodes and never lost site of the Creator. How egotistical is that? What Conrad was trying to show me was that my book could be about showing the reader how we may grow through adversity and pain.

I had to be vulnerable, perhaps for the first time in this particular way. I had to give up self-protection and move beyond fear of what others would think about me when they learned the details of my past.

I had to write my life.

And in the process, something interesting occurred. As I wrote about them, my experiences came to life—in Technicolor—yet I was able to see them as a spectator. Yes, I still felt the pain and the sadness, ugliness and stupidity, but I saw them with the clarity of hindsight. As I looked back on my past, I saw, not a collection of bad memories and tragic mistakes, but a succession of experiences, each one teaching me something new. I also saw myself, a flawed person who nevertheless managed to learn from her life, to grow in spite of her pain. How beautiful it was! Then I remembered Conrad's words:

"The raw stuff of life *is* beautiful." I have a choice. I don't have to see my past as flawed or ugly anymore. This too, is in the eye of the beholder.

Reflections

When you believe in the good, you can achieve the best. But believing in the good can be hard to do when you're on a journey through darkness, your only companions degradation and despair. Our first instinct is to protect ourselves, to stop and take cover. Even after all I had learned, when Conrad suggested I step forward into the light and make myself vulnerable, I hesitated.

But I saw that he was right, that perhaps something good could come from sharing my story. I walked ahead into that "new, scary place. This book is the result of that walk.

You, too, can meet your own challenges with confidence and conviction, even when they seem overwhelming. Meet them with understanding and compassion, and trust you will come out the other side whole and improved.

I know this can be done, for I have done it. When life hands you suffering, pain, or adversity, this does not mean those circumstances must dictate your worth. It is possible for you to wring success out of that pain. Challenges give us the opportunity to meet our own vulnerabilities head on. And sometimes, adversity can be a signal that it is time to do a little self-examination.

If we embrace the notion that something greater than ourselves is co-creating our destiny with us, we would probably view our experiences differently. We would view them as part of our training, as if we were getting in shape to run a marathon, or as course work in studying for a professional degree. What if we trusted that the universe (or God, the creator or spirit) always acted in accordance

> *with our highest good? What if we simply surrendered, held out our arms and allowed our hearts to remain open, accepting each experience as it came?*

QUESTIONS:

1) When has a decision to move forward towards a dream been hampered by the ego protecting you from exposure or failure?

_____

_____

_____

2) Is there room in your life to look at the rough patches with acceptance and forgiveness?

_____

_____

_____

3) What challenges are most comfortable for you: physical or emotional?

_____

_____

_____

CHAPTER TWO

FIRST DUMPING GROUND

*Quiet anger that implodes is as destructive
as rage that explodes.*

They didn't have to have us. We were lucky to have been chosen. If they hadn't rescued us, we would have been living in an orphanage, or worse—thrown out with someone's trash.

Yes, this is what our parents really told us, and often. The one thing we knew for sure about ourselves was that we had been discarded at birth. And at any point we could be discarded once again.

They also said that being adopted made us special, but really what they meant was that they were.

Look at us! We adopted these two little children, aren't we generous and kind? It was the mid-1950s, an era when adoptions were in vogue, made popular by celebrities like Joan Crawford. My mother—by whom I mean my adoptive mother who raised me—was often compared to Joan Crawford. She had glamour and a big, flamboyant personality. She also had some of Joan Crawford's less desirable attributes.

In front of company, my parents showed my brother and me off as though we were prizes they had won, and now owned. They said all the right things, like the birth announcement I still have, in my mother's handwriting:

On the 13th of May
Jimmy's 4th Birthday
A special girl has come our way
Come look for yourself
She is like a dream
Join us and you'll see what we mean

But the right things they said were really just for show. We were for show, like a new car that was kept sparkling clean and polished, although no one ever changed the oil.

Their ownership was underscored by our names. My brother and father were both James, my mother and I both Mila. "We gave you our names," my mother would often say sternly, to remind us that we had none of our own.

My parents' recurring line was, "We didn't have to have you." If we slid down the stairs on our butts, we'd hear my father shout "Don't break anything in my house—we didn't have to have you," reminding us that we were guests in his home. If we touched the walls with sticky fingers, "Don't bring your filth into my house we didn't have to have you, you know." If we spilled something on the carpet, "You're lucky to have a roof over your head—remember we didn't have to have you."

Aside from those words, I remember little else of my father from my early years. He was almost a non-person to me, fading into the background behind my mother's overwhelming clouds of emotion and non-stop drama. But it was clear that he adored my mother, as much as his flattened personality would allow. Maybe he had no energy left for anyone else. What he had left for my brother and me was mostly disapproval. When he had to be around us, he acted as though he smelled something faintly rotten somewhere and was waiting for it to dissipate. It was clear that the only reason he agreed to adopt us was because my mother said she wanted some children. And what my mother wanted, she got.

My mother was a dynamic woman who in many ways was ahead of her time. She was a professional photographer who owned her own business, in the 1950s when women just didn't do that. I don't think she was financially successful, but that didn't matter one bit, since my father's role was to be the provider. He had worked his way up in the San Francisco business establishment, and by the time I was born in 1956 they were well-off. I'm sure that's why she married him, for the security and stability he provided. I doubt she really loved him. She never made any secret of her extramarital affairs, which my father accepted with passive resignation, as he did with everything she wanted.

Besides Joan Crawford, she was also often compared to Lucille Ball and Gypsy Rose Lee. She had limited social skills and would say anything that came into her head, immediately after it arrived there. She was blunt, tactless and outrageous, and she loved scenes. Her taste in dress was shocking too, especially in the mix-and-match tidy fifties. She liked garish muumuus and she'd throw on any combination of garments, regardless of whether the pieces went together in style or color. To her credit, she was also enormously generous, both with money and with her time. If someone came into her studio with a problem, even someone she barely knew, she would go to work trying to fix it, coming up with schemes that were rarely practical, but always creative. (In fact, it was through "fixing" one of her customer's problems that she adopted me. Although I would not learn that until much later.)

Her flamboyance masked some deep-seated needs for belonging and stability. She was raised by carnival people, and if she had family I never met any of them. Perhaps that's why she was so insistent on adoption. She wanted someone to belong to her.

When she did things, she never did them half-assed. She did them big. Like the way she "loved" my brother. Their tortuous relationship was at the heart of our household.

Like me, Jimmy had been adopted, four years before I was born. (In one of those weird coincidences, we were both born on May 13th.) I don't know where she found him, or how she was allowed to adopt a baby. I'm quite sure she would not have passed any social services agency application. But she adopted him somehow, and she was determined to never let him go. All the clichés about the smothering mother were true about her. She called it love, but really she suffocated him with guilt, need and obligation; he too heard, over and over, "You'd be dead without me—we didn't have to have you." Jimmy had severe asthma as a baby, and his medical problems encouraged my mother to over-comfort and over-protect him. She kept him home from school and away from other children at the slightest excuse, "protecting" him right out of getting an education or socializing with his peers, until he became only marginally functional, even as a child.

I was schooled religiously in the doctrine that Jimmy was special and must be treated differently than all other people. The main reason my parents adopted me was to be Jimmy's playmate and companion, and to take any blame away from him. My job was to make him look good. Many years ago on Southern plantations the rich white children were given black child slaves for this same purpose. That's where the term "whipping boy" comes from. That's what I was. I was Jimmy's whipping girl.

My mother worked hard to keep me from shining in my own way, lest I outshine Jimmy. She even hid my report cards. I was a good student in grade school, always getting As and Bs. Jimmy didn't do as well, probably because my mother kept him home so much. So when I would come home excited with a good report card, or a paper that the teacher marked "Excellent," my mother would grab it out of my hands and thrust it out of sight, in a drawer or in the garbage, so Jimmy wouldn't see it and have to feel bad. "Shhh!" she'd hiss at me, before I could share my triumph.

When I was eight and Jimmy was twelve, our home life dramatically changed. My mother got sick. For the next four years she would be hospitalized off and on with a series of illnesses. But just because she was gone, that didn't mean that the family still didn't revolve around her. When she was home, she was confined to her bed, and we were all, even Jimmy, expected to wait on her. My father especially chained himself to her, and he never gave any sign that he resented those chains. I think he may have even liked them.

When she was in the hospital for protracted periods, my father visited her daily after work, and I often didn't see him before I went to bed. He had always been emotionally absent; now he was physically gone as well. In order to visit her bedside each morning, he left the house very early, so I didn't see him in the mornings either. Jimmy, left abruptly on his own by our mother's "desertion," started to hang out with his new teenage friends he'd met somewhere, so he was gone as well.

From the age of eight until I was twelve, I got my own breakfast, did my own laundry, made my own lunches, cooked my own dinner, and had no adult supervision at all. If I wanted to go to school, I did. If I wanted to watch TV, I did. I didn't tell anyone about my day at school or the programs I watched. Who would have asked? We lived in a nice suburban upper-middle class house, but it was like death there. And when my mother came home for short stays, before she retreated to the hospital again, there was chaos, and I was still alone.

I have few memories from this time, although I do remember watching The Donna Reed Show and wondering when I would find that family harmony and affection that the rest of America enjoyed. When I was nine and ten, I comforted myself by watching Donna Reed, wrapping myself in that half-hour of motherly love. But when I began to enter early adolescence, Donna Reed lost her power to calm me. Instead her show just made me angry because I didn't have what everyone else did.

I had always been curious about my birth parents, even when I was very young. But my parents never answered my questions. Or rather, my mother answered them differently each time I asked, so that it was impossible to know what was true, or if anything was. It was a waste of time talking to her about it. And after she got sick, it was impossible. My need to know who I was simply wasn't that important to anyone.

I told myself stories about my "real" family. I fantasized that they lived in Beverly Hills, that my biological mother was somebody rich and famous. This was when The Beverly Hillbillies was a popular show on TV, and I watched it every week. The hillbilly Clampetts were so out of place with the rest of Beverly Hills and that is what it was like in my life. Only in my world my mother was a Clampett and I was the one who was out of place in her world. She wore muumuus and slippers and would go out in public with her hair in curlers—she just didn't care. But even when I was a kid I had a flair for style, and I paid attention to what I wore. I color coordinated the clothes in my closet, so they looked good not only when I wore them, but also while they were hanging up. I put my toys away where they belonged—each one had its own place. But my mother piled her Reader's Digest magazines up in the corners of the living room, and left them there until they grew cobwebs.

As I entered adolescence, my curiosity and my need to find my true identity became a near obsession. All teenagers, of course, go through some trauma developing their identity, but for adopted kids it's intensified. I was plagued by unanswered, and seemingly unanswerable, questions. My lips were large; did this mean I had drops of African blood? I experienced early puberty; did this mean I was of Latin descent? I had developed breasts by the age of eleven and looked like a young version of the voluptuous Sophia Loren; did this mean I was Mediterranean?

No one would tell me. One day, my mother would say I was Greek, then another time she'd say I was French. She told me she found me by the side of the road and didn't know what I was. She told me my birth mother gave me to her because she already had too many children. (Ironically, this turned out to be close to the truth. But I didn't find that out until I was grown.)

From the moment I started kindergarten, I fantasized that my biological mother watched me every day as I walked to and from school. I pictured her looking out a window in the building next to my school, or hiding behind the big tree on the corner of my street. And she'd just be watching over me, checking on me to make sure I was doing okay, or because she missed me, longed for me, just like I longed for her. If a car would drive slowly past me as I walked, I would always wonder, is that her?

It's funny, for as long as I can remember, I've been told I am "unforgettable." I always stood out, maybe because I learned that to be heard at all I had to put myself out there. Whenever my class in school got in trouble, or was congratulated on doing something well, I was always the one picked to go to the front of the room. So my question was, if I'm so unforgettable, why did all four of my parents forget about me?

Reflections

As an adopted yet still unwanted child, I faced unkind and rough beginnings and grew into a young woman with sharp edges. My early life taught me to approach life lessons from the position of a rebel with anger as a weapon. In time, I became a warrior—a person always at war. I was at war with myself and the circumstances that brought me into this world. I would wear the warrior's shield well into adulthood, and even today it remains a readily available default position. It became my go-to tool; the one I used whenever I felt unsafe. Which was nearly always.

I will always remember the feeling that plagued me during my childhood—if only I fought harder, looked longer, I would find the place where I was truly wanted. It remained beyond my grasp for so many years. Disappointment left its scars on my heart. As a result, the lessons became even harder to see. Sometimes the pain felt like acid running into my heart.

When I recall those experiences that produced the scars, it is so easy to get pulled into the pain and reject the benefits. Life presents events that illustrate joy and pain. Our evolution depends on these encounters. However, we don't have to label events as good or bad, just accept them as purveyors of life lessons.

I recognized that I had to reframe my experiences. I had a warm heart, a sharp mind and compassion for self as well as others. These were my gifts. The question was how I could use my gifts to get through the pain? I no longer focused on lack but the talents I possessed.

> *I learned the art of forgiveness. Without forgiveness I would remain in bondage and could not move forward. I needed to see the blessing in not having parents who provided a structured upbringing; that I didn't have the standard "Do's and Don'ts list" that parents pass on to their children. Formality and shoulds may restrict and encumber. My parents' absence was an open canvas to create who I would be.*

QUESTIONS:

1) What are your memories that bring you pain?

___

___

___

2) Other than remembering these events, are you attached to re-experiencing this pain through your adult life today? Re-creating experiences that deepen your original wound?

___

___

___

3) How does this play out, manifest for you?

___

___

___

4) How does it feel to imagine forgiving anyone and everyone who ever hurt you?

_____

_____

_____

5) What would your life look like if your past pain was your biggest blessing?

_____

_____

_____

6) What did your pain teach you and how can that be a positive asset in your life today?

_____

_____

_____

_____

_____

7) How have your difficulties made you a better person?

_____

_____

_____

CHAPTER THREE

FAR BEYOND CONTROL

*Understand your motives before you act.
If you are guided by fear, selfishness, or retaliation—stop.*

When my mother underwent her third major surgery, I thought, this time, she really might die. I was twelve, nearly thirteen, and although a part of me was scared, another part of me was indifferent. And a third part of me (a tiny part with an, angry voice) thought, "Ok this could be relief—no more being haunted with the what if she doesn't make it."

By then, having no one home seemed like an advantage instead of a problem. At least that's what I thought, in all of my adolescent wisdom. No one told me what to do. No one stopped me from doing what I wanted to do.

My body had developed early. I had developed full breasts and started my period two years earlier. When I waited for the school bus, men passing by in cars would slow down and gawk at me. Sometimes they honked or called out "Hey, Honey!" which fascinated me. I had no idea why they acted that way, but I did like the attention.

By twelve, I knew more about what was going on in those men's minds. I remained drawn to the attention.

My childhood came to an abrupt end sometime before my 13th birthday. Hungry for a place where I belonged, where someone would value me, I started hanging out with kids at school who, like me, were wounded inside. The most important of these friends was Nancy, a smart-mouthed girl who craved a sense of belonging as intensely as I did. Nancy was what was then called a "mulatto," a term that has little meaning now, but which spoke volumes about who you were, or weren't, back in the '60s. Mulatto was half-white and half-black, which meant Nancy didn't fit anywhere, not in the white community where she lived, but not in the black community, either.

We met in seventh grade, outside the dean's office at school, waiting to be disciplined for smoking pot. The dean suspended us both, and we marched out the front doors together, our chins pointed high, our arms linked. We left, and went directly to score more pot and get high.

We were initially attracted to each other because we had both been branded as "bad girls," but we bonded through our pain. We were both broken. It wasn't long before we were hanging out at the beach together, getting drunk on Ripple, (a cheap, fortified wine popular with alcoholics in the '70s), or Boone's Farm Apple wine and crying as we shared our life stories. She cried about being molested as a child, and fitting nowhere because she wasn't black or white, and I cried about being all alone and not knowing who I was at all.

The big difference between Nancy and me was that she had a real family. It was a dysfunctional one, but in a totally different way than mine. My family life was filled with neglect, silence, and unspoken (though implied) hostility. Nancy's family life included abuse, and the hostility was right out in the open. Still, her family cared about each other, and if they showed it in unhealthy ways, at least they did show it. I started to hang out more and more at Nancy's house, and when we weren't there, we were arm in arm, exploring the heart of San Francisco's black neighborhoods.

I felt drawn not only to Nancy's family's warmth, but to the black community as a whole. Martin Luther King's assassination was still a fresh memory then, and many people remained discouraged by the lost promise of a dream. This was exactly how I felt about my own lost dreams. I found the plight of black people a hardship to which I could relate; I identified with being relegated to the back of the bus. I too felt isolated and disconnected from the "normal life" portrayed on television and sold by social conventions, and no one here had a Leave It To Beaver life either. So I aligned myself with these extended families on "the other side of town" because I saw that they stood together in bad times and good. I wanted to be part of their cohesive experience. I was too young and naïve to realize that my white skin and inborn yet unearned social privileges might be viewed with resentment by those same black people I felt connected to.

Nancy and I spent more and more time hanging around in the South Park neighborhood, an underbelly area of shanty houses, where drug dealers hovered in doorways and addicts got high on park benches just outside the local playground. My ongoing presence there sparked interest, especially in the adolescent boys. A white girl in their neighborhood was a novelty to them. If you were gutsy enough to venture into that neighborhood, and you weren't the cops, you earned your passport. It wasn't long before I was approached by an older boy—he was nineteen to my thirteen, so to me he seemed safe and sophisticated. We talked for a while, then started kissing, which escalated into groping and touching. He took me back to his family's apartment, and into his bedroom, where the fondling continued. Even with my limited experience, I had a vague idea that I was about to experience love-making—and that's what I thought it would be. I thought we would literally make love, and that meant he loved me, didn't it? I wanted to believe so, but I had been rejected so often I wasn't sure. I asked him timidly if he really liked me, and he tried to reassure me by saying, "Baby, you're fine." He also told me not to worry, that no one was home and we were safe. Safe was another one of my favorite words. So I took off my clothes and surrendered my body, even without a mention of love. Maybe love was too much to ask for; maybe being wanted was enough.

It didn't take long, and it didn't really hurt. Actually it felt good to be so close to someone. But that didn't last long either. After he finished, he got up quickly, and as soon as he did, the closet door opened. Three more boys were inside the closet, giggling and pushing their way out. They had been waiting for their turns—with me.

I struggled and tried to leave, but the more I fought the rougher it got. They outnumbered me four to one. So I submitted again, but this time only with my body. The rest of me, my soul, went numb. This is how I first experienced sex.

Although it seems incredible to me now, at the time, I told myself that the episode proved those boys believed I was worth having. After all the boys were finished with me, we sat around and got stoned together, pretending that everything was okay. The guy who started it—my would-be "boyfriend"—reassured me that I was his girl, and this was the way things were on this side of town. Things are different here, he said. Well, that at least was familiar—for me, things had always been different.

Today, we would call it what it was—rape. But back then, that word was virtually unspoken. The sexual revolution was in its first flowering, and everyone was trying everything they could with everybody, and trying not to pay the price for any of it. In fact, we all denied there was a price.

But of course there was a price, notably for girls. Most people routinely blamed rape victims for the crimes committed against them, in fact calling rape something girls "got themselves into." And this would be especially true if it happened between people of different races, or if the girl was assaulted somewhere she had "no place" being. If I had complained, it would have only made my life worse. The kindest question I would have faced would have been, "Well, just what were you doing on that side of town?" And even at my young age of 13, I knew this to be true.

This experience drove me deeper into unacknowledged anger. I couldn't tell anyone what had happened to me, and besides, I believed no one would care. Although I was rarely home, my parents didn't miss me. They only acknowledged my existence when I caused trouble, and the school complained. They clearly didn't want to be bothered, so I didn't bother to consider them either. I kept my pain to myself and sought comfort from the attention of more boys from the South Park neighborhood, who were always willing to comply.

In the fog of pain that ensued, going to school was agony. It made a mockery of me, throwing in my face the families, friends and love that I lacked. It was easier to fit in with people who had nothing, so I quit going to school. After seventh grade, I dropped out. I was fourteen and my life consisted of doing drugs, hanging out on the street—the wrong side of the street—and sleeping around. I was rarely home and when I was I ignored anything my parents said or did—if they were there—or I told them how I felt about them in less than civil terms. I was accountable to no one.

Until the city authorities got hold of me. Until the late 1960s it was legal to arrest juveniles for being "Beyond Parental Control" and to send them to Juvenile Hall for correction. I had committed no crime, but I was rightfully deemed to be out of control and I found myself placed in San Francisco's Juvenile Hall.

Already angry, it infuriated me to be labeled as "bad." But inside Juvenile Hall, for the first time I felt protected. I had something

I'd always longed for, a structured routine I could count on. You knew what was coming and when. You knew what was expected of you. You knew what was forbidden. You knew where you belonged. Inside Juvenile Hall, I was compliant and even friendly with the guards.

I was relieved and I was freed from my fragmented family and I no longer had to be concerned how I measured up—or how I didn't.

Perhaps if I had just stayed in Juvenile Hall for the next four years until I turned eighteen, my life would not have taken the downward turns it did. But that was not how the system worked. Juvenile Hall was a short-term solution. There were counselors, who were compassionate but stretched thin. They were as attentive as their limited time allowed, but in those days, the idea of actually counseling delinquents, trying to treat the underlying problems that caused their behavior, had not yet caught on. In their eyes, you'd done what you'd done, but there wasn't any need to look at why you did it, or to find a way to help you through it. They just wanted you to get over it and move you on through; perhaps they thought just being there was supposed to shock you back to good behavior. And then they sent you home with your parents.

In my case, of course, this didn't work very well. My parents had no authority over me after leaving me alone for so many years, and outside the structure and security of Juvenile Hall, my rage returned and I became even more defiant than before. After they learned they could do it, my parents would pick up the phone and call the police to come and get me when my behavior annoyed them, or when I disappeared for long periods. I cycled in and out of Juvenile Hall several times, until I returned home from a stay there to discover that my brother Jimmy had developed an unsettling obsession with me. His own anger and silent suffering led him into a dark place. He was binge drinking, and had developed some deviant behaviors, which my mother blamed on me. "He misses you when you're not here," she said.

When I told my social worker about the incident, the state removed me from my home the next day. The courts deemed my parents unfit and made me a ward of the state.

I suppose I could have taken some satisfaction in my parents being labeled as unfit, but the only emotion I truly felt was anger. I was back at Juvie, only this time instead of waiting to be released "home," I was waiting for placement in a group home.

My second home, with Nancy and her family, still existed as the only source of comfort and loyalty I had. Whenever Juvie released me to my parents, I usually headed straight to Nancy's home. And while I was in Juvenile Hall, waiting for the state to find a place for me to go, Nancy grew tired of waiting to see me. So Nancy would deliberately get herself arrested and sent to Juvie so that we could spend a weekend together. Nancy's family even tried to get a foster license so I could stay with them. But the system preferred the foster families they already had, and they rejected Nancy's family's attempts to bring me into their home.

The court assigned me a Placement Officer, whose job was to find a foster or group home for wards like me. Mine was Barbara, and I was lucky to have her. For one thing, she liked me. She thought I was smart, and she told me more than once that I could run the program. I liked her, too. She was in her mid-thirties and attractive—the male Probation Officers all liked her. She drove a Mustang, one of the coolest cars at that time, and we spent hours in that car together, when she'd drive me to placements, and we'd talk. She was quick, no-nonsense and a bit abrasive. Just like me.

But Barbara was a stop-gap, not permanent. It wasn't her fault that the group homes she placed me in never worked out. I was still too angry and too defiant. I had long since learned that my anger gave me power, that I could use it to keep people at arm's length, where it was harder for them to hurt me. Naturally, this meant they couldn't help me, either. I ran away from three group homes, one after three weeks, one after ten weeks, and the last one after eight months.

When I ran away, I didn't go to my parents' home, which wasn't home to me anyway. Sometimes I'd drop by there to get some clothes or some money, but that was it. I never stayed. Instead I'd hang out on the streets during the day, dropping a little acid, smoking a little pot. At night I'd crash at Nancy's, or another friend's house, if they had a spare couch or a room in their garage, or just a space on their floor. Until I got picked up and sent back to Juvenile Hall again, to await a new placement.

Self-abuse was the most common theme of my life on the streets. Even though abuse at the hands of others occurred over and over, I believed that I was the one who allowed it to happen. I was raped more than once, although I didn't call it that. Each time, I made my body numb and the incident into a non-event that could not hurt me.

The word that best describes how I felt about myself is disposable. My birth mother disposed of me. My adopted parents disposed of me. Juvenile Hall disposed of me. It was Barbara's job to dispose of me. So what if I allowed the boys I slept with to dispose of me too? At least it was familiar.

I never thought about what I was doing or where I was going because I thought I'd be dead by twenty-five. I mean, who would want to live longer than that?

Reflections

Sometimes we ask ourselves, "Is this all there is?" The answer is always no, even if we don't know that at the time. Our next question might be, "Where do I go from here?" The world answers you by bringing you circumstances that make you question your purpose, asking you to go deeper.

Understanding who you are is the beginning of moving purposefully into the future, rather than just "hanging in there." This shift in perspective allows for transformation.

To live powerfully we must first begin to live in trust. To experience the abundance of possibilities awaiting us, we must disengage from our righteous stance in our past survival skills.

Today, I know that taking action from a place of fear is the surest way to fall into a deep hole. I wish I had known that as an adolescent, but teenagers are not big on self-knowledge. My motives were unclear and confusing to myself and others. I didn't think about why I did what I did. I was afraid, angry, lonely, and wanted to act on those feelings. I made others the bad guys so I wouldn't long for their company. Today, I choose to shift to a platform of possibilities.

When how we live our lives becomes more about respect for life and less about what we can take out of a situation, we can be free of the narrow-mindedness that once limited us. Living in fear of potential circumstances discourages self-love. This limits the opportunity to experience joy. Fear through control actually promotes the very thing we're trying to avoid.

Fear constricts, castrates, and ultimately kills the beauty of what is. Once we decide to live with intention we begin to live

> *purposely, casting off the corseted constrictions of previous events. We can believe in laying out a welcoming mat, a trusting place, for opportunities.*

QUESTIONS:

1) What specific actions have you taken in your life because you were afraid? Lonely? Angry?

_____

_____

_____

_____

2) What was the outcome of those choices?

_____

_____

_____

3) Are you making anyone in your life the "bad guy" right now?

_____

_____

_____

OVHS

4) If you shift your perspective to what the "bad guys" have to teach you, such as, "They are pushing my boundaries so I can learn to stand up for myself," what life lessons are you being taught from these good guys?

_____

_____

_____

5) Who do you believe yourself to be at your core? What are your three best qualities?

_____

_____

_____

_____

6) How do you let the world see these characteristics?

_____

_____

_____

7) How could you shine more?

_____

_____

_____

8) Recall an experience when you did your best and trusted life to show you the next step. What was the outcome?

_____

_____

_____

Do something today that shows your motivation is love not fear Journal about the action you took.

_____

_____

_____

_____

_____

_____

_____

_____

_____

_____

_____

_____

_____

CHAPTER FOUR

WORKING HARD FOR THE MONEY

We all have an Achilles' heel that shows us where we are limited and need the most work.

―――

When you need to learn something, your teacher will appear. But there's no guarantee your teacher will be good and kind, or that learning will be some sort of glorious Aha. Some of the most effective teachers are monsters, and the lessons that teach you best are the ones that cause you the most pain.

I was just seventeen when I met Gene. It started out as a normal day; I was doing my usual thing, which was nothing except floating around looking to get stoned. In the morning, I'd gotten high with a guy I knew slightly, one of the other drop-out kids, and my plan for the afternoon was to take the bus to Market Street and shoplift some new clothes. After that—well, after that was too far ahead for me to think about.

I was waiting for the bus at Haight and Fillmore when a gleaming Cadillac El Dorado, so polished it nearly blinded me as the sun bounced off the chrome, pulled up in front of the stop. The driver, a sophisticated-looking black man, leaned out the window and looked right at me.

"Want a ride?"

His voice was deep and smooth, like velvet. Trying to be cool, I said "Sure," and got in the front seat. I breathed in the rich smells of new car, leather, and spicy aftershave. Beneath my cool exterior I congratulated myself. "You go, girl!" I thought. I had caught the eye of an obvious "somebody," an amazing thing—what would a somebody want with a nobody like me? I didn't argue with such good luck. It didn't come my way very often.

Power and command oozed from him. He introduced himself as if his name were famous. He looked a little like Sammy Davis Jr., only bigger and more handsome. But his air of cool and style was the same. His hair was slicked back, his clothes and his jewelry looked expensive, even his nails were manicured. He was obviously a lot older than me, so it didn't cross my mind to think he'd be interested in me sexually. I thought he was just being nice, or had some time to kill. Yeah, I know, I was naïve as hell. Just because I had lived on the streets did not make me street-smart. But I was about to take a crash course.

Right away he started asking me questions, not just about where I was heading, but about what I thought, what I'd seen, what I'd done. I told him I was going downtown, but we hadn't gone more than a few blocks when he asked if we could take a little detour, go somewhere we could talk. It was the first time in a long time that anyone had cared enough to ask to talk to me. He listened, too. He seemed to find me fascinating. I said, "Yeah, sure," and we drove up to Coit Tower, where he parked like he had all the time in the world to spend with me.

We stayed up there for hours, just talking. "Baby, you are just too young and pretty to be out here wandering around," he told me. "What do you do all day?"

When I told him, laughing, that I'd dropped out of school and just hung out with my friends getting stoned, he didn't laugh with me. "Why would you do that?" he asked, staring right into my eyes. "A pretty white girl like you, you can have anything you want. Why do you want to throw your life away?"

His deep, strong voice, so soft and full of care, his intent looks directed right at me, and only me—it was hypnotic. He encouraged me to talk, tell him everything, and once I started, I couldn't stop. I told him about my parents who weren't my parents, and how they gave up on me and were glad when I was taken away from them. I told him about Juvenile Hall and shuttling between there and the street for the last couple of years. I told him about boys who lie and say "I love you" and then before you know it, they're letting their friends take their turn with you. I talked and cried, and cried and talked, as though I were confiding in a long-awaited girlfriend, pouring out my grief for a life that had been just one crushing disappointment after another.

He listened intently, shaking his head in sorrow and disbelief, never taking his eyes off mine. He seemed so gentle, yet strong and confident. He could help me, he said, it troubled him that I was so sad and lost. He kept repeating, over and over, "You don't see what you've got, right in front of you. You can have anything you want. You don't see how lucky you are, the world is waiting for you. Let me help you."

In a couple of hours I was hooked. Gene knew all about me. I knew little about him. When I asked what he did, he was vague and brief. An entrepreneur, he said, a businessman. That sounded okay to me; I didn't really care. What was important was that he cared for me.

It was getting late, and he invited me to have dinner with him. Dinner in a real restaurant—a new experience for me. I felt awkward but dazzled when he took me to Fisherman's Wharf, and ordered crab for both of us. Rich people did that. It's not what I did, or ever expected to do. And through it all I talked and he listened, periodically telling me that I could have anything I wanted, the whole world was open to me.

I finally asked him how. What did he mean I could have anything I wanted? For years, I drifted from one place to sleep to another, from one shoplifted outfit to another, from one cadged meal to another—never knowing where the next one was coming from. It was ludicrous to say I could have anything I wanted. He was nice, but he must be crazy.

"I'll show you how tomorrow," he said.

I was happy to hear he wanted to see me tomorrow, but I still didn't believe him. "Yeah? What are we gonna do, rob a bank?"

He laughed, and then said seriously, with that intent look of his, "I promise you, it's nothing like that. Nothing you'd go to jail for. I'll show you how tomorrow."

I wanted so much to trust him. So I did.

That night he took me to a luxury high-rise hotel out by the airport. "You're a classy girl," he said. "You should have a classy place to sleep." Already, I was getting used to his flattering remarks. I had stopped thinking "Who, me?" every time he said something nice. I had started to really like those compliments. Maybe even need them.

When he told me I had a beautiful body and he'd like to spend some time with it, I was surprised but flattered. He was so much older, so much more sophisticated. I felt safe in his presence. Sex meant little to me; it was a small price to pay for his protective warmth. Why not sleep with him—what did I have to lose?

Sex with Gene was so different than my other experiences. For one thing, there was no "Oh baby I love you" that I would hear from the boys on the street, which I knew by then was a line of shit. Because Gene didn't lay that particular lie on me, it made me trust him more. Also, he took his time, no in-out-done. He focused on my pleasure instead of his own. I had never had oral sex before that night, and it was a revelation. I fell asleep in his arms.

The next day he fulfilled his promise to show me how to live the good life and have everything I wanted. He pointed out that I had been giving away part of myself—my body—and getting nothing in return. It was time to take control, he said, and profit from what I had to offer. I was a young, pretty white girl, worth a lot to those who would pay. And he would show me how—what to do, what to say, where to go.

"It's easy," he said. "Nothing different than what you're already doing—except now you'll be making money. Lots of it."

I said I'd give it a try. Why not? I did not know then that "giving it a try" was not an option. I didn't know I had signed up for slavery.

Gene was a thorough teacher. He showed me how best to display my assets, how to select and screen the johns, how to ask for the money, get the money, do the jobs. And how to stay safe—from the johns, the police, and the rival hos he called "Ladies of the Night."

He showed me where to stand, on a corner that belonged to him along what was called the "Ho Stroll." He told me to ask for "twenty five and $3" which meant $3 for the room and $25 for the actual deed. These days, of course, it would be more like fifty and five. I was to stand on the corner and when a guy pulled up I was to walk up to his car and say, "Hey you want a date?" Sometimes you'd have to say more, like "Want a half and half? Straight sex or blow job?" I was amazed at all the lingo I had to learn. This was the hardest part for me—to ask. Instead of them coming on to me, I had to come on to them. That was what felt weird.

And then there was the actual job. Gene showed me where to take the guys who wanted a date. There were lots of housing projects around our corner, and you could always find some old guy who was a drunk, or was on disability and lived alone. They made their money by renting out their rooms as so-called "trick pads." The old guy would sit in the living room watching TV. I was to go in and give him the $3, and take the john into the bedroom. I'd get a washcloth and wash him, then wash myself. I'd give him a condom, and we'd do the act. That was it. Gene said it shouldn't take more than five to ten minutes, max. Then I'd go back to the corner.

That first night, from 10 p.m. to 3 a.m., Gene watched me from the window of a 2nd floor apartment across the street from my corner. I was glad he was there; it meant I was safe. After the first trick, he congratulated me, saying "Good job! The next one will be easier." He was right, because after the first couple, I did feel pretty pumped up. I could do this!

And at the end of the night, I had a couple hundred bucks. Whoa. This was a piece of cake. And Gene was proud of me. He told me he'd take care of me from now on, and the first thing we had to do the next day was get me a place to live, and then in a few weeks, after I'd made enough money, he'd get me a car.

A place to live. A car. I thought I'd died and gone to heaven.

He warned me, though, that I'd have to work hard. Every night. And man, did I work. I probably did at least fifteen guys in those first few days. I worked my ass off, so to speak, and in no time at all I had $1,500, the most money I'd ever seen in my life.

The money all went to Gene, of course, but I thought it was mine. After all, he spent most of it on me. He got me an apartment on Upper Market Street, just like he promised—although it was in his name, and he let me know he could come and go whenever he wanted, with no warning when he'd show up or when he'd leave. He took me down to a furniture store and bought nice furniture for my new place. He bought dishes and rugs and everything I needed, all good quality. When we went into a store, the salesmen fawned all over him. I thought it meant they respected him, and because I was with him, I felt like somebody, too.

And my God, the clothes he bought. We went to the Polk Street boutiques, and a leather shop in North Beach, and he watched me try on clothes for hours. He thought nothing of dropping $100 on just one dress—and in 1973 that was a lot of money. Then he would buy shoes and a purse to match the dress—made by Gucci, of course. At that time I did not know Gucci from Walgreens, but I learned fast.

After we went shopping, he'd take me out to dinner. I'd wear my new clothes and we'd go somewhere expensive, and he'd teach me how to behave in a nice restaurant.

And then I'd go back to my place and get ready for the night. I can't say I liked the work—it was sometimes distasteful, often boring—but I didn't mind it that much. I could see with my own eyes what it bought me. Shopping in Union Square for designer clothes, ordering the most expensive thing on the menu at world famous restaurants, all those things that only "other people" got to do—well, it worked to fill my empty soul.

Most of all, the work gave me "my man." Gene cared about me, paid attention to me, doted on me. He even gave me the nickname, Punk. I'd never had a nickname before and I took it as another sign of his affection. Oh, I was proud to belong to him, and when he praised me, I felt valuable for the first time in my life.

CHAPTER FOUR

The big awakening came about three weeks later when one night I was tired, sore and just felt raw inside. The last thing I wanted was to put anything up there, and I was starting to feel harnessed. But, after the first few days, Gene didn't stand and watch over me anymore, rather he would drive by my corner every now and again with no warning, and as he went by he'd give me that look. The look meant "Are you doing what you're supposed to be doing?" He cross-examined me at the end of my shifts, especially if I didn't bring back enough money. "Weren't you looking? What were you talking to some chick instead?" I would try to explain, but no explanation covered the sin of "not enough." And lately, he hadn't been buying me much. He just took the money. In short, I wasn't having fun anymore.

I told him I wasn't going out that night. And he took off his mask. His deep voice went deadly cold.

"Who do you think you are, to tell me you're going or not going?" he said. "I own you. You are mine."

I was stunned. Own me?

"What?" I said.

"What do you think is going on here?" he snarled. "You go when I tell you to go."

I still didn't get it. I argued. This was a mistake I didn't make again.

"No, I won't," I said. "I don't want to do this anymore."

"No? No? Let me show you how 'No' feels."

His rage filled the room like a black cloud. On the stroll, we called it an "ass-kicking," but that doesn't begin to describe it. He threw me against the walls. He used his fists, his shoes, whatever he laid his hands on, to beat me. He hit me on my head, my neck, pulled out my hair, stomped on my skull, stepped on my chest. I was stunned by the lengths he went to hurt me. He had no limits. He knew every way there was to hurt a body, every way that would leave no visible marks that a john could see.

It seemed to go on forever, and when it was over I was a different person. I didn't belong to myself anymore. I belonged to him.

When I went out on the stroll that night, the girls looked at me and said, "Yeah, you were turned out." That's what we called it, turned out. It's when you understood what you had gotten yourself into. And that there was no way out.

For the next year and a half, I worked the Ho Stroll, every night except Sunday, from 10 at night until 3 in the morning. The Stroll was an area of three or four blocks in San Francisco's Fillmore District. You stood on the corner that your man owned. After Gene turned me out, I learned he had more than one girl. He owned three of us. I was the only white girl. In fact, I was the only white girl on the Stroll. It made me stand out more, so I always got business. And I was dependable, always there. Gene made sure of that.

After awhile, I didn't even need to solicit as much. The guys knew where to find the trick pad, so I could come out of doing one guy and another one would be waiting in the living room. I reeled them in pretty quick, and since it was never more than ten minutes from start to finish, I could do 7-8 guys a night. There was never any fondling, caressing, tenderness. Kissing was strictly off-limits; foreplay unnecessary, a waste of time.

Most of the johns were blue collar workers—mechanics, janitors, and UPS drivers. Nearly all of them were married. The girls on the stroll used to talk about the women who were married to these guys. We called them "flat-backers." We had no respect for them. In our wackadoodle thinking, we thought they were doing exactly what we were doing, only they were owned by husbands, and we were paid so we were free. God, what lies and stories we tell ourselves in order to make it through.

I worked the Ho Stroll at the height of the terror caused by the Zebra killings. For more than six months, a handful of men stalked San Francisco, murdering 15 people and wounding eight others. The killers turned out to be Black Muslims affiliated with the Nation of Islam, who called themselves the "Death Angels." They targeted white people in the hopes of starting a full-on racial war, and they chose their victims at random. San Francisco police responded to the killings by treating practically every black man like a suspect. The whole city, it seemed, dwelled in anger and fear.

As someone who spent every night standing on a street corner, I felt especially vulnerable. And the killers came close, shooting one of their victims right down the street from my corner. I heard the gunshots. I was terrified, but I stayed where I was, huddled in the doorway of a Laundromat. I was so afraid of Gene giving me an ass kicking that I decided not to leave. I preferred to take my chances with the Zebra killers, rather than risk setting Gene off.

The hardest part of every night was right at the beginning. You had to "break luck," which meant your first date or trick. (If you were decent to a guy, you called him a date. If you talked shit to each other, you called him a trick. Although you'd never say "trick" to his face.) After you broke luck, you could start racking them up, but the first one took some mental manifestation. If you broke luck early, you could relax and know the night would be a good one. This upped your confidence, so when you approached the next trick you looked better to them, and they'd respond and want you more than the other girls.

If it was midnight and you hadn't broken luck, that was a bad thing. It meant you only had two hours to catch up. The last run was the guys coming home from the bars at 2:15 to 2:30 a.m. Closing out the night with only $75 or $100 was just not worth going home. According to the pimps, if you couldn't break luck, it was your fault. You must have been doing something stupid, because if you were dressed right and out there and willing, you would be screwing everyone who drove by. It was simply unacceptable not to break luck. You knew if you didn't you would get your ass kicked.

If the night was going good and you saw the cops coming, you'd stand back in a doorway so they'd pass on by. Sometimes you'd give them blow jobs and they'd move on. But if it was nearing midnight and you hadn't broken luck yet, you'd rather go to jail than go home. So you'd stand on the sidewalk when the cops came. That was called "obstructing the sidewalk," and the cops would pick you up if they needed to meet their quota. A couple of times when I was on the Stroll, the cops came by in a paddy wagon, which meant they were doing a sweep and picking up everybody.

It sounds strange to say this, but the sweeps were sort of fun. In that life, you had to find fun wherever you could. No one was afraid of the cops. They were just doing their jobs. They'd come by in the paddy wagon and open the back door, saying, "Hey we gotta do it, picking up the quota." And the girls would pile in. A couple of times we stopped at a place called the Doggie Diner on Van Ness, and they'd let us get something to eat on the way to jail. The next morning we'd go into court and they would dismiss the case. It was a game we all played.

Going to jail didn't always work to avoid an ass-kicking; it usually just postponed it. The couple of times I got picked up, Gene demanded to know why I "let myself" get arrested. My answers never satisfied him, because he already knew the answer—I wasn't working hard enough. And that meant when I got home I had an "ass kicking" waiting for me.

For the first few months after my "awakening," he beat me every night to underscore that I was his property. While beating me, he told me what I was to earn, how I was to treat him, and when and under what conditions I was allowed to come home.

Almost worse than the beatings was Gene's ability to keep me off-balance, always on high alert. I never knew when or where he would show up. Maybe on the stroll, where he would just slowly drive by and look at me. Or it would be at five in the morning and I would be in my apartment in bed and suddenly he'd be there, staring down at me. Or I'd be at home on Sunday night, the only night I didn't have to work, watching Sonny and Cher on TV, and he'd jump out of the closet. It took me some time to understand that he had his people keeping tabs on me, so he always knew where I was and what I was doing. Sometimes when he'd unexpectedly arrive, he'd be very complimentary; other times he beat me, because he said I was slacking off. Or because he said I was mouthing off. Or because I was getting too comfortable. Or just because he could. But then, sometimes he wouldn't.

I was Gene's trophy servant, a person with no identity of her own. Gene took to calling me "Gene Jr." to underscore his ownership. I always had to sit in the back seat, and I was never allowed to speak to him first. When we slept together, he kept me dependent on him by playing my body like a violin virtuoso, giving me orgasms that he made sure I understood were to be kept only for him. During sex he would repeat, over and over, that I was his and I could only come for him. He was the only man I was allowed to kiss.

I began to believe I could endure anything. I had no dignity; my need to survive abolished it. Surviving left no room for any luxuries—such as happiness. In fact, I no longer knew what happiness was.

My entire life was Gene. No one else mattered. I had no friends, except for Nancy, who I still saw once in a while. But Gene disliked her; she threatened him because she was the only person I was still connected to outside the life he had made for me. I had to sneak around in order to talk to her, and if Gene found out, it meant another ass-kicking. And mostly, he found out.

Sometimes I went to see my parents, although our relationship had not improved at all. In fact, my mother liked Gene. She thought it was time someone could control my behavior. It meant she didn't have to think about me at all. As for my father, I disgusted him. He knew what Gene was, what I was, but true to form, he didn't say much about it. Except, when I'd leave the bathroom, he'd yell at me to spray the toilet seat with Lysol.

As for the other girls on the stroll, we didn't become friends. It's not like you see on television, hookers with hearts of gold looking out for one another. We were competitors. Who was dressed the best, who could catch the most dates. Especially, we watched out for our man's interests. We might warn each other about psycho johns we'd been with, or when the cops were out in force, but that's it. If someone got an ass-kicking, no one had any sympathy—no one said, "Oh too bad, are you okay?" Instead we said, "What did you do?"

Compassion is a weakness on the street. You can never show it, because it will take you down. After a while—a short while—you don't feel it. Not for anybody. Once you start to feel for someone, you'll start to feel for yourself. You might have to acknowledge what your life is. And that's something you cannot do, ever.

You might think I hated Gene because of the abuse, but I didn't, at least not then. I feared him, more than I feared anything, but I also thought I loved him. He was "my man," who took care of me, who paid attention to me. I paid attention to him, too. I knew what was important to him and what wasn't. His family meant little to him—his mother was a timid woman who worked as a hotel housekeeper and could barely keep her life together; his father was an older version of Gene. His girls were important to him, though. We were the source of his power, status, and money. Just look at me: in my Gucci, minks and diamonds, I was a luxury-laden Barbie doll, the personification of the only thing that meant anything to Gene, money. He admired other successful pimps and Muhammad Ali for the same reason—they made money so they could tell the white man to fuck off.

Gene didn't always treat me bad. Sometimes I thought he actually loved me—it was me and him against the white man's world. Gene and I had similar views about what life was like in that world. It wasn't life at all—especially without money. So we needed each other. He kept me safe from the world, and I made him enough money to tell the world to go to hell.

That we were the ones living in hell, well, we never mentioned that. It wasn't safe to think that way.

Squares, as we called anyone not in the life, always ask the same question—why didn't you leave?

Yeah, right. Leave—and go where and do what? I was clearly marked as damaged material. I saw it in the eyes of the squares when I walked alongside my pimp. I knew what they thought of me—the same thing my parents thought, that I was somebody you wouldn't let in your bathroom. There would be no help coming, no safety, no protection, if I left Gene. I'd be totally alone. With Gene, I belonged to somebody. Yes, at a cost, but at least somebody was invested in whether I lived or died. What did I care if his motives were wrong? Here, finally, was a person with a reason to stand for my existence.

Reflections

For a human being to survive, he or she must have a sense of belonging somewhere, to someone or something. As children, very few of us are secure and wise enough to know that this belonging is our birthright, and that we can never lose it. So we equate our survival with belonging to our parents, our family, our friends—something outside ourselves. If this need is not nurtured when we are young, we are going to find it somewhere anyway, because the basic need of every human being is to survive.

If you live in a continuous state of danger, where nothing and nobody is safe and you belong nowhere, you will go into acute survival mode. When you're in this survival mode, you're so pumped up and into qualifying every situation and every person who comes into your orbit as dangerous that you don't really experience what "is". You certainly don't feel your soul. You exist at a primal level of operation.

This fight mode can become a way of life. You become addicted to the adrenaline coursing through your body. It begins the moment you wake up. You scan for possible threats to your survival. You constantly figure out escape routes and alternate plans. You are on Red Alert, living in the Red Zone.

In the Red Zone there is no room for other possibilities. Those things that may be warm, kind or happy are discarded because you have no room to enjoy them. Your only focus is on the dangerous possibilities that may exist, and how you will prepare for them.

QUESTIONS:

1) Where in your life are you merely surviving, instead of thriving?

_____

_____

_____

2) What steps could you take towards thriving and changing things for the better?

_____

_____

_____

3) What fears keep you stuck in your "comfort" zone?

_____

_____

_____

4) Have there been role models in your life who challenged the status quo, left a bad marriage, a frustrating job situation? Do you have friends who you can talk to for inspiration if you want to get out of a circumstance that is no longer fulfilling?

_____

_____

_____

_____

5) Imagine your ideal day from morning until night. What are you doing? What are your triggers? What are the pet peeves that upset you over and over again and cause you to create drama in your life?

_____

_____

_____

_____

6) On most days do you live in the Red Zone, where there is no room for possibilities? Or the Yellow Zone, where you see options but are too cautious to move forward? Do you prepare for the worst by focusing on your fears or worries? In your daydreams, visualizations and journaling, explore what it would be like to live in the Green Zone, full of fulfillment and possibilities.

_____

_____

_____

_____

_____

_____

_____

_____

CHAPTER FIVE

CLIMBING UP WHILE GOING DOWN

Set your bar high, but retain your flexibility, so you can adjust when necessary to accomplish your end goal.

I got pregnant with Gene's child about six months into my new life. But according to Gene, this didn't mean I could stop working—many customers liked the anomaly of a pregnant girl, so business didn't slow down much.

I was not the only one. A lot of girls on the Stroll were having babies. The pimps encouraged it. When Gene slept with me, he didn't use a condom—another thing I didn't think much about. Gene wanted me to have a child, but I didn't grasp that, nor would I understand why until after my daughter was born. She became Gene's hostage, too, and another means for him to keep my chain short and iron clad.

But there was another reason Gene wanted me pregnant—money, of course. The pimps wanted their girls to have a child so we could get on the AFDC, the Aid to Families with Dependent Children, government program. The girls would collect a regular check, which of course went right to their pimps. I didn't question it, as Gene told me that's just how things were done, and watching the other girls living the same way made it all seem normal.

Few girls had more than one child—it was not like anyone was trying to create a family. A pimp didn't need more than one child to keep his hook in you. In fact, more children may have required more of you than they were willing to sacrifice. Gene understood what I did not yet know, but soon would—that most girls, damaged as we were, would love our children. Most of us would have done anything to keep our kids safe. Out there on the Stroll, you could see girls doing just that—anything—to keep their children safe.

Gene also encouraged me to repair my relationship with my parents. His ulterior motive, of course, was so they would take care of the baby after it was born, freeing me to keep working. It was an uphill job with my mother, because we still despised each other. But she allowed me to build a nest inside my childhood bedroom, where I hadn't lived for years. The closer it got to my due date, the more things I packed into that room—bassinet, blankets, diapers, bottles, stuffed animals—all for the little baby doll I thought I was having.

I was 17, a baby myself in so many ways, tethered to a dangerous man, living a dangerous life, and about to have my first born baby. For many months, it didn't seem real to me at all.

My water bag actually burst when I was with a trick. Nobody told me I shouldn't be having sex so close to delivery. The trick was a regular, so he was okay with it. I just jumped on a streetcar and went to the hospital. On the way I took some painkillers, because I figured labor would probably hurt. When I got to the hospital, I was really out of it. I kept screaming, "Give me something for the pain!" but the doctors refused because they weren't sure what other drugs I was on. Instead, I had a "natural" childbirth, but I don't think there was much natural about it. I gave birth to my daughter surrounded by strangers wearing scrubs, and without the loving support from a partner or a mother or a friend, something most of the other women on that floor had.

But Erica's arrival in the world quenched a thirst I'd carried my whole life—to share a bloodline with someone. My first born daughter was my only known blood relative.

I was surprised—and yes, grateful—when my parents and brother came to see the baby and me in the hospital. It was my mother's doing; neither my brother nor father cared one way or the other. My brother didn't say one word, and my father's only comment was "She's awfully dark." But my mother was a force. When my father made his racist comment, my mother elbowed him in the ribs. She wanted this grandbaby, and the color issue disappeared the minute she saw Erica's beautiful face.

I think by this time my mother had come full-circle in her life. She saw how much she had missed with Jimmy and me because of all her illnesses. She had also recently suffered the first of several strokes she would have, and she was looking for another cause in which to participate. She saw her last chance in Erica.

Gene picked Erica and me up from the hospital and deposited us at my mother's house, where I would recover from the episiotomy. Even he seemed to realize I couldn't have sex right away. From the time we got there, my mother was on board with being a grandmother—she never did things halfway—and this time I thought it was cool. Taking care of Erica was the first thing we ever did together, and those early weeks at the dawn of Erica's life were the first time I'd ever had fun with my mother.

Gene started coming around within a week, to check things out. He shrewdly ingratiated himself with my mother early in our relationship, buying her little gifts and showering her with compliments. Also, he showed her how he could control me. On my own, when my mother annoyed me (which was often), my usual response was to say, "fuck you." But when Gene was around, he would shoot me one of his looks, and I would know to say nothing. My mother appreciated Gene; she actually looked forward to his visits. It was weird, but I let it go—what could I do?

He wined and dined me again, taking me out to nice restaurants, telling me I could leave the baby with my mother—who was delighted to have full charge of Erica, and also encouraged me to go. During dinner he'd wheedle me into coming back to work part time, saying things like, "You could just do afternoons, you wouldn't have to do nights," although I knew better than to believe him. I also knew that the wheedling would eventually turn into being dragged by my hair, if I didn't agree.

I was back out on the Stroll a few weeks after Erica's birth, and a month after that, I turned 18. I found out why Gene pushed me to come back so soon—I was in high demand because many of my regulars had come to appreciate the naiveté of my spirit. And they were willing to pay for it. During my absence, they kept asking where the pregnant girl was. People need to feel like they count—even if only in the commercial act of negotiating for sex with a virtual stranger.

I left Erica with my mother most of the time. I'd pick her up on Sunday and take her back to my apartment, where she'd stay with me until Gene picked her up on Tuesday morning and took her back to my mother's. Gene and my mother grew even tighter. The small beginning my mother and I had made in fixing our relationship withered away. I felt she and Gene conspired to cheat me.

I was back on the street, yet something in me had changed. Erica was the first person in the universe who I knew was truly mine. Because Gene had fathered her, she was a mixed-race child. In the

'70s being a mixed-race person was difficult. I saw how hard it had been for Nancy. I looked at my tiny innocent baby, and it hit me what I had done. The responsibility to nurture and protect her fell on me. Yet I was so vulnerable and confused myself. Oh My God.

My attitude toward Gene shifted, too. I wasn't as proud to belong to him anymore, although I still told myself I needed his strength. I was certain he would not abandon me, as long as I maintained my high profit margin. And of course I was still terrified. I accepted that I could not leave him, but I became determined to do things differently. My daughter gave me a reason to live; I no longer had the luxury of dying before I was 25. Somehow I had to convince Gene to let me stay alive—my way.

I knew that Gene's priority was money and money alone. If I earned more money, maybe I could buy my freedom. If slaves could do it, why couldn't I?

Gene told me repeatedly while courting me that I was young, pretty and white, that I could have anything I wanted. Now, I knew what he meant. I could blend in higher-class circles, where I could earn more, reduce my risk of getting arrested, work fewer hours and spend more time with my daughter. Without asking for Gene's approval, I decided to break into the world of call girls.

I said goodbye to the Stroll and staked out a new territory in the upscale hotels on Nob Hill and other fancy San Francisco locales. Before long, I was averaging $1,000 a night for just four to five tourists. In the '70s, this was a whole lot of money, and it quickly persuaded Gene to let me make the move, just as I suspected it would. My earnings tripled in just one month.

My newfound earning power gave me a little leverage in my relationship with Gene, and I used it to persuade him to give up his other girls. Pimps referred to their girls collectively as their "stable," and I'd always hated that. When you long for a family, you don't want to settle for being the prettiest pony in the barn. Erica's birth only intensified my desire to build a family, and I'd begun establishing what felt like one to me—Gene was my man, I was his only "girl," and together we had Erica. And I believed that being Gene's only source of income would give me more freedom, at least in the home I was trying to create. I planned to buy my freedom, but I wanted to play house until then, too. Sure, my thinking was twisted, but when you're living in the Red Zone, you savor what little freedom and family you can chisel out for yourself.

Once I moved uptown, the changes within me accelerated. My clients were no longer the mechanic on his way home from the bar, or the UPS man taking a break. The interactions didn't take place in dark and squalid back rooms. Now my clients were stockbrokers in town for a convention, or Europeans on holiday, or foreign businessmen making deals with their American counterparts. These men represented achievement, and they radiated confidence. As they escorted me to social functions, they treated me respectfully. They said "please" and "thank you." They asked about my tastes and regarded my wishes seriously. And something shifted, too, in my experience under the sheets. It became more human, less mechanical. It felt clean.

I began to recognize myself as someone of value. I no longer felt discarded. The more time I spent with these accomplished men, who enjoyed my company as well as my body, the more I began to see myself as their equal. I steadily outgrew the subculture of the street, developing some confidence and courage.

My Japanese and Arab clients especially impressed me, with their knowledge and experience, and our cultural differences fascinated me. I even learned how to speak limited Arabic, and as time went on, I developed strong relationships with some of my regular clients, notably Yoshiro from Japan and Fasil from Saudi Arabia. Men who pay $500 to share your body sometimes believe they can do whatever they want to it. Yoshiro and Fasil never made that assumption. I was fond of Yoshiro, who was always so courteous, and who I believe in his own way loved me. But I adored Fasil. He had confidence, strength, but most of all internal discipline.

He was different in that he wasn't a traveling businessman, like Yoshiro. He was a student, studying for his graduate degree at Stanford, so he would be around for months at a time. He was also extremely rich, connected to the royal family in Saudi Arabia. More than anyone else, he gave me a new sense of myself. He liked to talk with me, and we spent hours and hours doing just that. He'd tell me about his studies, and he'd talk about cultural differences, history and economics and literature—and he would listen to what I had to say about these subjects too, with respect. He often said I was way too good for the life I was living and actually encouraged me to quit the call girl life—after he went home for good, of course.

Once, when he went back home for an extended visit to Saudi Arabia, he sent for me. He stashed me in a hotel for ten days, visiting me every day. He didn't share me with anyone, I was there just for him, and he paid accordingly. Though I never left the hotel, that trip opened a new horizon for me. Fasil paid thousands of dollars to bring me half way across the world, just so I could be closer to him. No one had ever valued me that way before.

Yoshiro also paid for me to come to Japan, once for two weeks and another time for a month. I'd see him whenever his schedule permitted, and I augmented my trip by visiting Osaka, where the Caucasian drinking partners (that is what they called us) worked. It was a great opportunity to make a significant amount of money for little "work."

For all my worldliness, I was still a teenage girl, and these trips were scary. But they were not only lucrative, they were also necessary to survive in the call-girl profession. After a girl started working the fancy hotels, it didn't take long before the vice squad would be on to her. The vice squad didn't operate like the street cops, picking you up for obstructing the sidewalk and stopping by the Doggie Diner for a quick bite on the way to jail. Vice cops were callous, they saw you as their prey, and they would shut you down.

A vice cop would learn when you worked, your routine, and even your car—if he saw it parked on the street, he'd just go through the lounges in all the hotels in the near vicinity until he found you. He'd make your life miserable by following you, sometimes tag teaming you with one of his vice cop buddies, maybe even stopping your john and making you give the money back. And then he'd probably demand a blow job as his price for not taking you to jail.

There were probably about twenty of us girls working the big hotels for the two years that I was there, and every cop had his own favorite that he'd fixate on, and try to shut her down. To them, it was a big game.

The way I found to win the game was to take advantage of their rotation system, by going away periodically, and returning when a new vice cop was rotated in. I didn't just go to Japan and Saudi Arabia; those trips were special. Usually, I went to Vegas or Reno and worked there. I even spent a week at the Mustang Ranch once. Then I would come back home to San Francisco, give the money I had earned to Gene, and start working the hotels again, ducking a fresh batch of vice cops.

Gene hadn't disappeared. I had not been able to fulfill my dream of buying my freedom, because the more money I made, the more accustomed he became to having it. Still, he was slowly losing his grip on me, and he knew it. My success threatened him, even as he profited from it. I still paid him, of course—there was no way I could go to Saudi Arabia for a week and not come back with at least $10,000 for him. But I was smarter now. I didn't give Gene all the money. I kept some back for me.

Saving my own money was a terrifying act of bravery. I was so afraid Gene would find out and kill me. Then what would happen to Erica? He often said he would kill me, or kill my friend Nancy, or anyone else I loved, and I knew he was capable of it. He was progressively becoming more and more violent. The beatings got so bad I was afraid he'd cause me to develop a brain tumor, (he usually hit me repeatedly around the head). Once he evened knocked out my front tooth, and then after I had it capped—he knocked it out again.

Nevertheless, my confidence grew, and I began to make my first attempts at leaving him. I gathered my strength, and called Nancy, who was the only person I trusted. She knew what my life was, and still loved me. She had begged me for years to leave Gene, so she was more than happy to help plot my escape. (This is why Gene hated her, and more than once he pulled a gun on her. I tried to limit how often I called her, because I feared for her safety.)

The first few times that I tried to leave Gene, I was never successful for more than a few days at a time. Each time, Nancy would search out a place for me to hide, but Gene found them. I don't know how, but he always tracked me down. Just when I'd been gone long enough that I could almost relax, he would sneak up on me, jump out from behind a bush, or a garbage can, or a closet. Of course, he beat me unmercifully while eroding my soul with a constant degrading, and absolute demoralizing verbal abuse as well.

But it wasn't Nancy who finally convinced me to leave Gene for Good, it was Erica.

After I started making money as call girl, I moved out of the apartment on Upper Market and rented a nice little house. It had a yard and everything. Up until Erica was 10 months old, she lived with my mother, but once I got the house, I started bringing her home with me more often, and keeping her with me longer. This set off a power struggle with my mother, who didn't want to give Erica up. It was a struggle that lasted more than a year, because I couldn't just take Erica away for good; I still needed my mother to care for her when I was working. Once again, my mother and I argued every time we saw each other. I took Erica home with me as often as I could. Whose daughter was she, anyway?

But the more Erica came home with me, the more she saw how I really lived. She witnessed the beatings that Gene would rain down on me. Finally, one day after Gene had been and gone, I stood in the living room, sobbing, shaking, and bruised from head to toe. Erica, who was about two and half years old at the time, looked up at me and said, "Please don't cry. Why do you let him hurt you?"

That did it. Her simple question made it suddenly clear to me that I had created a volatile environment for this trusting little being, even more insecure than the one I had endured as a child. The hard truth went through me like a knife: This is not okay.

At that moment I knew I would leave Gene forever. That did not mean that I knew how I would do it, or how I would live with the terror if I succeeded.

But leave him, I did.

I had saved up enough money to last about a year. I sold my car, gave up my house, quit my profession, and basically dropped off the planet as far as Gene was concerned. Even today, thirty plus years later, I don't want to say where I was during that time. And Gene is dead now! Intellectually I know he's dead, but emotionally I can easily revert to fear. When I hear a door open unexpectedly, I start to shake because the unknown is on approach. Then I remind myself to breathe and let down my guard.

I lived in hiding for a year. You'd think escaping Gene would finally bring me peace of mind, but instead, I lived in constant terror.

As a little girl, I was so afraid of the bogeyman, I hid knives under my bed to protect myself. I grew up, and the bogeymen became real: teenage boys leapt out of closets and raped me; Gene burst into my room in the middle of the night to beat me; vice cops stalked me, lay in wait for me outside hotels, around darkened corners. Alone in my hiding place with Erica, it seemed that danger lurked everywhere. It would be years before I could look at a closed closet door without worry.

Fear dominated my life, but I fought it, mostly by staying high and intoxicated. It's a good thing I didn't have any tranquilizers, because I would have taken those too, and either killed myself by mixing them with alcohol, or becoming addicted. Gene never allowed me to do drugs, or even to drink. I was a prisoner suddenly set free. Without him around telling me what to do and not to do, I didn't know how to set my own limits. But the real reason I stayed high was that it eased the terror that stalked me. It didn't kill it entirely, though; nothing did.

After about two months, I took Erica back to my mother because I knew I was not fit to take care of her. I refused to tell my parents where I was living. My mother would have told Gene, I knew she would.

Only two of my former clients knew where I was. Fasil was one. He visited me and supported my decision to leave my old life, though he objected to my drinking and getting high. He simply didn't understand how deep my fear was, and that I needed to stay numb to keep it under control.

The other ex-client I let into my hiding space, I did out of necessity. Duke was a drug supplier. During my last year as a call girl, we got to know each other pretty well. He was a low-level member of a drug cartel; an experienced navigator, he smuggled drugs—mainly marijuana—into the United States by boat. He was also a fearless man who would do anything, who thrived on action and danger.

He partied hard, too. He ran with a crazy crowd of rock stars and other celebrities who had too much money and not enough ideas on what to spend it on. It wasn't unusual for them to rent a Lear jet and hire a bunch of us call girls for a week to accompany them to Vegas or Beverly Hills or Ann Arbor or wherever their whims took them. Like me, Duke depended on dangerous people to earn a living; and he had even less control of his life than I did.

Duke and I became friends during my year in hiding, although our relationship, though sexual, was never romantic. Ironically, it was my longing for structure and control that brought us closer. A few months after leaving Erica with my mother, I began to emerge from my zombie-like drugged state to evaluate the condition of my life. I wanted my daughter home with me, to give her a stable life, and to live my own life as a normal woman and mother. I wasn't sure what that meant, only that it meant getting off the street. The problem was that the only skill I had was one I no longer wanted to sell. I had to figure out a goal and come up with a plan to get myself there.

Despite his wild lifestyle, Duke longed for structure too, if nothing else for short periods of refuge. He was attracted to my single-minded determination to put some civility and stability into my life, and he offered me a way forward if I would take him with me. We made a business agreement to take care of each other. He'd support me financially in a nice home where I could live the life of an average, normal housewife and mother. And when he came home from his parties or his dangerous smuggling runs, I'd soothe him with my smoothly running home and complacent body.

It sounded like a great trade to me. I would achieve my goal of getting off the street. Duke had powerful friends, much more powerful than Gene, so Gene could no longer get to me. I would be normal. I would be average. I would be safe.

It would take many alterations to my goals before I would realize that the words normal and average were never going to apply to me.

Reflections

I believe that our ego limits our ability to be authentically human. It focuses only on protecting Number One. Acts of service toward humanity at large are outside the ego's comfortable scope. It is a shield of armor which discriminates as to what is safe to pass through and what is not. The ego has a strong need to protect our belief system; we create a sense of what is good or bad as we endorse what is comfortable and reject what is uncomfortable.

But ego alone, like any character trait, cannot be qualified as good or bad. It simply is. The ego can be used with wisdom and discrimination; it does not need to run the show. It can act as a barometer to identify when we are at risk. Ironically, those who are consumed by feeding the ego lead limited lives, because fear that is the undercurrent of the ego actually promotes our limitations.

Ego has a place in your life just as your big toe has a place on your foot. Your big toe is there for balance. If your entire wardrobe was created to highlight your big toe, you would be severely out of balance. Like a hungry gremlin, ego will consume everything in its path once you begin to feed it. The greatest attribute you can develop as a maturing person is development of the soul force within. The ego will come into balance and you will be able to maintain flexibility in setting your goals. You won't be consumed by the need to self-protect that is driven by fear.

QUESTIONS:

1) Can you identify people in your life who live from ego? Do they see right and wrong in black and white terms with judgment attached?

_____

_____

_____

2) Identify the grey area of a situation that you recently thought you were 100% right about.

_____

_____

_____

3) Does tapping into the grey area between right and wrong help you connect to your soul more than your ego?

_____

_____

_____

4) Do you feel more compassion for yourself and others when you look at life events from the perspective of the grey area?

_____

_____

_____

5) Do you ever try to get what you want by manipulation? How do you think it would feel to instead ask, not demand, for what you want?

6) How frightening or freeing does it feel to think about putting your ego aside and be vulnerable? Journal about it.

CHAPTER SIX

A WITNESS TO CHANGE

Every place I arrive is a destination I charted myself, with my own decisions.

I found my duties to be pretty easy in my new quasi-business relationship with Duke. He was like a merchant seaman, his merchandise being marijuana. He was gone for four months, home for six weeks, gone for three months, home for two weeks. My job was to stay home, play house, keep my legs crossed while awaiting his returns, then greet him with a friendly, well-stocked oasis called home. Given the life I'd led before this, being on standby didn't seem harsh; it was peace. Duke was an intermittent aberration in the life I was trying to make for myself as a mother. I had reclaimed Erica from my mother, and soon learned I was pregnant again.

I hadn't tried to get pregnant; in fact I was using a diaphragm so I was shocked, but not unhappy. Although abortion was now legal, I never even considered it. I wanted more kids. I was less concerned with who the father was than having the child. My own father was so completely detached from my childhood—I didn't think the role of the father was terribly significant. Erica was my daughter before I recognized Gene as the father and he was worse than Duke. A pot smuggler was a notch up from a man who claimed ownership of me. Whatever Duke did for a living was fine with me, as long as he didn't beat me or discard me. I asked that he keep what he did away from me and my children. I did not see him capable to fulfill his role as father to the baby I was about to have. Traditional roles meant little to me, living as I had until then for sheer survival. Now I had the image of a functioning family, and I did not want Duke's brief appearances to threaten that illusion.

Oh, I was full of denial. But the thing about denial is you don't know that's what you're doing. I thought I was making a good life for my kids. I taught Erica, now 5, to read. I took her to the park and on play dates. I enrolled her in Montessori school, and you can bet I went to all the parent-teacher meetings. I read books about parenting and the stages of infancy and childhood. By the time my second daughter Tara was born, I was fully committed to being a successful parent. Like her big sister, Tara was a beautiful and special baby, and I was overjoyed that, this time, I would get to be a parent to her from the beginning.

Good thing too, because Tara was only a couple of months old when I got pregnant once more. Again an unplanned surprise, and again I was delighted. More people who were related to me—wow! More chances to prove to myself that I was good at something normal.

Yet all the while, the foundations that supported this happy dream were crumbling underneath me. A few months before my third child my only son, Ryan, was born, Duke came home looking worried. "They're closing in on us," he said.

At first I ignored him. I thought, "Whatever. These guys take themselves way too seriously." I barely listened when he talked about smuggling, the risks he took in his adrenaline-fueled life, or the guys he worked for. The corruption and danger didn't seem real to me; it was like a TV show that you forgot as soon as you turned the set off.

It got real, though, and fast. Days away from my delivery date, Duke informed me that he believed our house was under surveillance. Drug Enforcement Agency officers had been painstakingly tracking down every member of the smuggling ring, interviewing their families and friends. They had already interviewed my parents by now. "We gotta get out of here," he told me.

He wanted to leave (where we would go, he did not say), but how could I go anywhere when I expected a baby any day? We would wait until the baby was born, but as soon as we could, he decided, we would relocate.

Ryan's birth passed by in a fear-laden blur. I now fully realized I had been playing house with a criminal, and my children had been supported by notorious drug runners who were committed to keep their operation alive.

Ryan was not yet three weeks old when the DEA agents burst into our house. Maybe they knew we were on the verge of splitting. They crashed through the door and made all of us—including 5-year-old Erica, 16-month-old Tara, and even baby Ryan—lie face down on the floor, guns pointed at our backs. I lay there listening to them ransack our house, and fear gripped me once again, heart and soul.

This terror was different than any I'd experienced before, infinitely worse than anything Gene put me through. This time I wasn't afraid for myself: I thought they were going to kill my children. I lay with my face pressed to the floor and my arms encircling my crying babies, and I prayed to a God I had never believed in before.

They took us away in separate cars—Duke in one, me and my children in another. While they interrogated Duke, the children and I waited in a featureless room. Finally a couple of agents came in and told me that Duke had agreed to provide information against his former colleagues, in exchange for two years in a "security camp" instead of fifteen years in a federal prison. They said that while we waited for the trial to start, to protect Duke's testimony I would have to enter the Federal Witness Protection Program and remain there for an indefinite period of time. Otherwise, my children and I were in danger of being kidnapped or harmed by the powerful Colombian drug cartel Duke would be ratting on.

They were very convincing and I feared the Feds far less than I did Duke's cartel, so I agreed. I had no idea what to expect, but my beautiful housewife-mother dream had quickly been shattered and revealed for the fake that it was. I had nothing else, and anyway, all I cared about was the safety of my children.

The DEA sent us a thousand miles away, and for the next seven months we moved from one Midwest hotel to another. We went to all of the "M" states; Michigan, Minnesota, Missouri. I'm sure this comment maybe unfair to those states, but, in my opinion these states were chosen because they were the most boring, colorless places that could be found.

And cold. It was autumn (and later winter) and I was totally unprepared—we were California people. The first place we went—I think it was Michigan—I left our hotel room to go shopping for diapers or something, wearing spike heels, jeans, and a tight t-shirt. It was snowing. The kids' coats were thin, and they started shivering. I had to buy sturdy shoes and boots, coats and mittens, stuff I'd never owned before. I bought myself a down jacket that totally hid my shape, which felt so weird because I'd come to rely on my looks and now you couldn't see anything beyond my eyes. If I wasn't a blonde with a hot figure and a designer wardrobe, who the hell was I?

Every hotel room they moved us to had beige walls, beige carpet and windows overlooking parking lots. They always had two double beds—one for me and baby Ryan, and Tara and Erica in the other. I moved the furnishings around to make room for the kids to play. I got pretty good at improvising with pillows. Every few weeks, federal Marshals would give me about 24-hours notice to pack up and get the kids ready to move, because they were going to take us to yet another hotel room that looked pretty much the same as the last one, even if they were 800 miles apart.

My only human contacts were hotel maids, front desk people, and my babies. Federal Marshals stopped by about once a week to give me my stipend for food and diapers, but I wouldn't call that human contact. They were all business, seldom made eye contact and it was obvious they had no regard for me. They always came in pairs, and they never communicated through phone calls. They'd just stop by at irregular intervals. I've never seen such unremarkable looking men. They could blend into any crowd, and you'd be hard put to describe their faces. I could describe their clothes, but only because they all wore windbreakers—same color, same style. They never volunteered any information, and certainly never made any personal comments. If I asked a question, their answer was always the same: "We'll ask the department and get back to you."

I created a schedule of activities to structure our days: in the morning we'd do exercises for an hour while watching a fitness show on TV; then I'd give the kids a bath; then the maid would visit and I'd stock up on toiletries. If it wasn't snowing or raining too hard, I might take the kids on a walk outside, but usually we would just end up taking a walk around the hallways. We would go to the hotel restaurant for an early lunch; if we went before noon it was less crowded and then we could interact with the waitstaff a bit more. That would be our social outing for the day. This also allowed me to get more mileage from my funds by eating two meals a day rather than three. I used the money I saved to buy coloring books, games and puzzles for the kids. After lunch we returned to our room for playtime—Erica would solve math puzzles or read her books, Tara would color pictures or do simple jigsaw puzzles, and Ryan would play with rattles, kick his legs and arms, and practice sitting up by himself. He learned to crawl in those hotel rooms—it was a red letter day for me when he first inched his way across the floor. Then the kids would take their naps and so would I. After nap time we'd play some more or maybe we'd take a cab to the local market and buy a treat; then we'd go down to dinner. After dinner I'd read to them, we'd watch a little TV, and then we'd all go to bed.

I tried to focus all my energy on my children. I celebrated every little triumph—"Look at you crawl! You can say bye-bye! Oh my God, look what you can do!"

But outside of the children, too young to provide adult distraction, it was quiet in those hotel rooms. At first my paranoia was intense—I was scared all the time—and I couldn't numb it with pot anymore. Being sober, all of the monsters from my nightmares started coming to me in broad daylight, while I was wide awake. Closets, garbage cans, an overgrown shrub, all once again heralded danger. Who would jump out and attack my children and me this time?

But as time went on, the monsters faded and it gradually dawned on me that I was safe. I didn't have to be on high-alert. It was in this stillness that I found what I never had before: space and time to know myself.

Into the space came the questions. How can I get out of this life? How can I make our lives better? How can I not be on high alert all the time? In time, answers were revealed.

Those bland hotel rooms always have one thing in common: a Bible. I opened one, and read—and re-read—the Sermon on the Mount. The words of Jesus gave me hope that I was worthy of love.

Then on one of my weekly shopping trips to buy coloring books and diapers, I found a book authored by Louise Hay. There, I discovered that I could love myself.

They say you don't know what you don't know. Because of those two books, I began to let go of old thoughts and attempted to learn what I did not know. "What you give out, you get back," Louise Hay said. What? Did she mean I already had the power to change my life? Could it really be as easy as making different choices? Did I feel confident enough to become something I didn't know how to be? Could I make choices without a guide? How would I know if the choices were right? Up until now I just let life happen and did my best to roll with the punches.

The stillness of my life in Witness Protection allowed me to finally hear the quiet words of encouragement. But it would take more than quiet to make a change. It would take courage and faith in something I could not see. And I still did not fully understand.

Jesus' words conveyed to me I was loved. It would take time for me to totally believe it, yet just the possibility comforted me. Louise Hay's words showed steps towards how to believe it. In those bleak hotel rooms, my life began to change. From the inside. The place where foundation is formed

Reflections

When you live on the streets you are always in fight mode. Flight mode does not exist. Flight to where? Everywhere is dangerous. You live on high alert because if you don't, you're dead.

When you're on high alert you don't have the space or the time to think deeply about anything. You don't wonder why you chose this life. What a stupid question; by the time you figured it out your life would be over.

When you're on high alert you don't have the space or the time to know yourself. Instead you learn how to hide yourself. Otherwise someone will get you. On high alert, you're always ready for something bad to happen.

It's not fun to live on high alert. It took being in the Witness Protection Program to teach me that I had chosen to live that way. High alert isn't fun, but it is colorful. It is busy; so busy that you don't see the lessons right in front of your face. So busy you don't hear God talking to you.

Thank God for the Federal Witness Protection Program. The space and time I was given, the safety, and the relief from high alert allowed me the insight that I could make a different choice. I was the one in charge.

But I didn't have to do it all alone. God was with me. In fact, God had been there all the time. I just hadn't been listening. Now I was.

Not everyone would call the Federal Witness Protection Program a miracle, but I do.

QUESTIONS:

1) The sayings, "Hindsight is 20-20," and "God's rejection is for your own protection," can prompt us to look back at our life and recognize miracles protecting us when our own vision was short-sighted about what was taking place. What are examples of this hindsight in your own life? What has been your own Protection Program?

_____

_____

_____

_____

_____

2) Name your angels; the people in your life who have showed up to help, protect and guard you along your way when in difficult circumstances.

_____

_____

_____

_____

_____

CHAPTER SEVEN

IT'S NOT JUST ME ANYMORE

Relationships are required if you want to thrive.

A lot of people have found God when they are down on their knees. That didn't make me special, and it didn't mean God promised to make the rest of my life go smoothly. I knew God was not going to heal me while I just sat around and did nothing. What I learned in those isolated hotel rooms was that I was in charge of the actions that would promote healing. If I wanted to change my life, I had to make better decisions and change my responses to events. As simple as that.

I started making new decisions right after Duke testified and was given his brokered sentence. The Feds wanted the kids and me to change our names and move permanently to the Midwest, to keep us safe from retaliation and revenge at the hands of the cartel, which of course still existed despite the DEA's efforts.

I said no. I wanted to go home to California, and I even missed my parents, especially my mother. Besides, I was through with running because of my fear. I was through having other people tell me who I should be. I decided to define myself, and to live a life of dignity. I needed to teach my kids to be effective in the world, and how could I teach them if I couldn't do it for myself?

Sounds good, doesn't it? But as with all learning, it doesn't progress on one smooth upward line. You learn a little, you fall back a little, you learn a little more. It is a cycle of living. But I was determined, that with each step back, two more forward would follow.

At first, in my desire to give my kids a "normal" life, in a settled home with a father in it, I decided to be a good and loyal "wife" and wait for Duke while he did his short stint in prison. I moved us back to California, and we occasionally visited Duke.

In between visits, I began building a new life for me and the kids. Meanwhile, I still hadn't learned to love myself completely— I sometimes worried that I would slip back into old patterns of impulsive short sighted survival, but I worked fiercely at keeping my feet planted. I knew I had to get fully healthy. Although I didn't really know what that entailed, I did know that I had to protect my kids.

The fear that stalked me all my life pressed down on me again in those months. After all, I now had documented evidence, courtesy of the DEA, that someone wanted revenge for Duke's testimony. And I'd stepped out from under the shield of Witness Protection. Sometimes, it was hard to gather enough courage to walk my children to the playground.

But on my 25th birthday, I forced myself to leave the house. My mother volunteered to watch the kids, and I took myself to church. There, I contemplated surviving to 25, an age I thought I would never see. I contemplated my children, the family I'd longed for. I marveled at my new-found realization that life was precious, my life was precious. And from there I began to view life as a gift rather than a burden. I was filled with gratitude. "Thank you," I whispered in the hush of that church. "Thank you. Thank you. Thank you."

We were getting along okay until Duke got out of prison and moved back "home" with me in the Bay area. Prison hadn't changed him the way Witness Protection had changed me. He was still the same—addicted to adrenalin and only happy when he was living on the edge. He had no boundaries, no structure, and absolutely no judgment about the kinds of people he let into our lives. I had to stand back and say, "Whoa! Somebody's got to be the adult here."

There were no real adults in sight. When we became parents, Duke was 32, I was 24, and neither of us had much idea of what responsible adults were like. But someone had to step into that role, so I did. I took the kids and left him, choosing to be a single mother. For the first time, I had to learn how to live without a man to define me. I was scared to death that I'd fail, but I had to try for the kids because they were what my whole life was about now.

Learning to be a mother is always on-the-job training, for everybody, but usually moms have somebody on whom they can model their parenting. The only thing I was sure of was that I could not do that. Even though my mother and I were still working on patching up our relationship, she was the last person I would choose as a role model.

To be honest, I learned how to be a mom from television. I had been an "All My Children" junkie since the age of ten, when I started playing hooky from school to watch daytime soap operas instead. I still watched them while in the Witness Protection program, and even named my children for the strongest characters—Erica, Tara, Ryan. Sounds silly, I know, but actually, it wasn't. Those characters on TV were my family. I could count on them always being there, at noon every Monday through Friday. When I named my kids after them, it was a concrete representation of my hopes that we would always be there for each other. I tried to create a solidarity I had never before known.

From TV, I gleaned ideas on what parents and kids could do together. I took my kids to the park, and I'd push them on the swings. I took them to the zoo and to the beach to explore the tide pools. We caught minnows in the river. We would have had a dog if I'd had stable housing. All the images I saw around me on TV and in the movies, or even in the advertisements—they were my teachers.

The most important thing I tried to give my kids was structure, which was the big gaping hole in my childhood. No one had been there for me, no one cared or was involved in what I did with my days, or whether it was good for me. I was left to find my own way, with no guide and no tools. I yearned for structure because I was so alone and angry inside. Left to my own devices, with limited tools, I would self-destruct, as I proved over and over again. The only places I had structure and where I knew the rules, were in Juvenile Hall and later, with Gene. I swore to myself that this would not be my children's experience, that they would not flounder all alone, or be reduced to getting what they needed from the government or a group of misfits. In short, I was totally committed to being the parent I never had.

Continuing the routines I developed while we were in Witness Protection, our days were organized down to the hour. There was an hour for naptime, an hour for healthy snack time. Time to play, time to share, time to talk with each other. An hour for Sesame Street, an hour to read and then an hour to bathe.

I was always conscious that I was building these children into adult people. Every day I asked myself, "What do I want my kids to be?" I wanted them to develop the skills to contribute to the world in a positive way. I wanted them to have the tools to live a good and decent life. I saw it as my job to give them these tools. And I took it seriously.

I never allowed myself to feel lonely, because I wasn't alone—I was the leader of a pack, a pack of four. I remember the doctor asking me, after I'd had a difficult delivery with Tara, how many children I planned on having. Without even thinking, I said, "I want six." I was not focused on the role of the father. I wanted six kids because in my mind, that would be ideal. I wanted to be part of a powerful clan. I wanted to create a family group where we all had value, meaning and purpose and, most of all, where we all had one another.

I worked hard at introducing my kids to different kinds of people, and different experiences. I didn't try to over-protect them. Even when they were very little, I'd get them up from their scheduled naps and I'd set out clay, paints, crayons on the play table and encourage them to choose for themselves. I didn't choose for them.

As they got older, I organized birthday parties, sleep-overs, field trips for their schools, enrolled them in Girl Scouts and Boy Scouts. I opened up as many opportunities for them as I could find. Erica was in a band. She had wind-surfing lessons. Ryan and Tara were part of a ski club. Ryan went to a summer camp for indigent black kids, even though he was neither. I wanted my kids were all kinds of people. I wanted them to be able to handle every situation. It was really important to me to create people who were not dependent, who could think on their own, who would and could make a difference in the world.

All this effort was hard work, especially since I was making it up as I went along. Not everything went perfectly, no matter how much structure I set up. As Ryan grew beyond a toddler, I began to consider for the first time, how growing up fatherless would affect him. Who would teach him to be a man? With Tara, I fretted that as the middle child, she didn't get enough attention. She tended to take on too much, like a tiny little mother herself.

I really beat myself up over Erica. I felt so guilty about saddling her with a mixed-race identity in a prejudiced world. She experienced so much bigotry, so much blind anger and hate, so much sheer stupidity. In the early '80s, when she was only six, a bunch of white kids chased her all the way home, screaming "nigger" at her. That was a nasty scene—I reverted right back to my street personality and went after those kids, and after that their parents, who thought I reacted too harshly. In the end, I went to the school and took a stand about the racial harassment being heaped on Erica.

People nowadays forget what it was like only thirty years ago, even in the liberal Bay Area. We'd just be living our lives, trying to be normal, and suddenly a little thing would turn into something ugly. When Erica joined Girl Scouts, we bought her uniform at Sears. I bought the wrong sash—I bought a Brownies sash to go with a Girl Scouts uniform. So we had to go back to Sears to exchange it for the right one. I had Erica go into Sears alone to give back the old sash and get the new one, while Tara, Ryan and I waited in the car. It was such a production to take two toddlers into a store that I thought it would be easier. How hard could it be to return and exchange a sash?

We waited and waited, and she didn't come back. I couldn't imagine what happened. Finally, I had to pack up both little kids and go into Sears to find her.

They had her in a room where they take shoplifters. I had forgotten to give her the receipt along with the Brownies sash. When she tried to exchange it for the right one, they assumed she was stealing. She was eight years old.

It was so obvious that they assumed she was a shoplifter because she was black. They refused to listen to her explanation—with black people, there is only one explanation. When they saw me, their faces revealed everything they thought. First they were respectful to me, not realizing I was her mother. Then, when they understood, they looked confused. Finally they looked disgusted.

And she was so forgiving! She looked at my furious face said, "Mother, they just don't know what they're doing. They don't understand." From the beginning she's been like that, teaching me grace and acceptance through her elevated awareness of everyone's common humanity. She tolerated ignorance far better than I. And I thought I was the one who was supposed to teach her.

Looking back, I guess I was the epitome of the nauseating parent who talked on and on about her kids. My kids were literally the reason for my existence. They were both my source and my purpose—the beginning and the end.

As a single mother, I felt as if suddenly I had become emotionally responsible for the well being of "all my children." How could this be? I could barely handle my own life. I had not even begun to deal with the financial expectations, let alone life's basic requirements. All I knew was that it was me against the world with my mini-army close by my side.

Kids make you show up. Before you have kids, you can take a ticket and ride wherever you want to go. When you have kids, that freedom is no longer an option. After being on the street, I knew I didn't get to be stupid anymore. Although my fresh wounds were barely covered by new skin, I now had to live beyond the age of 25. The next decade required that I show up, competent, and ready to meet the needs of all my children.

Reflections

Relationships are required if you want to thrive. I became a parent three months before my eighteenth birthday. Finally, there was another human being with whom I shared a bloodline. I didn't concern myself with the role of the father, as I saw this as a small detail not worthy of consideration. I still lived like a delinquent, only now with brief breaks when I'd make my short-lived attempts to parent. But one thing was different—I no longer acted quite as self-destructively as I had in the past, since a child now depended on me to keep myself alive.

As the next few years passed, I finally began to mature. I started to see a direct correlation between the choices I made and the consequences I endured. I was empowered by a new-to-me reality: I had something to do with how things turned out.

I worked very hard to accept, and not fight, the position I was in. I came to understand that as a result of poor choices, impulsive behavior, a lack of self-regard, and the thrill of living in the face of danger, I created this destiny for myself—and if I wasn't careful, for my children.

I would not have had that epiphany if it had not been for my children. Until they were born, every relationship I had was founded on fear, domination, or neglect. I dimly realized that there was another way to relate to people, but it wasn't until I became a mother that I understood what this way was.

At the time I was raising them, I tried hard to make up for the gaps in my knowledge. I beat myself up for all that I did not know, and the mistakes I made. But now I know I was just learning, like we all are. What matters is that, finally, I created relationships based on love, respect and a commitment to a purposeful life.

When they were small, I was motivated by the need to protect my kids. I thought I was saving them. The reality is my children saved me. They are the people who taught me that relationships are what life is all about. Meanwhile, as challenges presented themselves I began to see them as God knocking at the door, calling me closer towards finding my faith.

QUESTIONS:

1) Who are the key people in relationships in your life that give you a reason/purpose to live your life better?

_____

_____

_____

_____

2) What have you learned about yourself from being in relationship to these key people in your life?

_____

_____

_____

_____

3) How have these relationships impacted you or caused to grow?

_____

_____

_____

_____

4) If you are a parent, write down how your children have taught you thus far what you have needed to learn about your life.

_____

_____

_____

_____

_____

_____

_____

_____

_____

_____

_____

CHAPTER EIGHT

SHE DID LOVE ME, AFTER ALL

*Needing love and approval from others is wasted energy.
Others come and go, but your self is always with you.*

My mother liked to rescue people. I admire her for that. If she saw someone, anyone, hurting or in trouble, my mother would work until she dropped to find a solution for them. Usually this meant her taking over. This is where my admiration stops. When her rescued "babies" didn't adhere to her plans for them, she'd drop them like they were scalding her. She dropped me when I was around seven or so, as soon as I began talking back and questioning the role she had assigned me as my brother's keeper.

She was such an all-or-nothing person, my mother. You were good or bad, right or wrong. There was nothing in between. According to her, I was not what she ordered from the adoption menu. This is why she knew that once I became a teenage mother my daughter, Erica, needed rescuing. My mother took over with Erica when she was a baby, and never voluntarily relinquished her or recognized me as the "mother."

In her defense, I was not a good mother when Erica was very young, even though I loved her and wanted to be a good parent. I was in distress, getting beaten regularly and desperate to save my child from the messed-up life I was living. Erica was better off with my mother, I knew. Given my opinion of my mother's deeply flawed parental abilities, this was a huge admission of failure for me to make.

My mother agreed with me about what a failure I was as a mother. She made sure Erica saw me that way too. "Your mother isn't coming back," she told Erica over and over, even though I always did. "Don't listen to your mother," she said, "She doesn't know what she's doing." She belittled me to Erica every chance she got. As a result, Erica didn't know who to trust. She always looked at me as if she was weighing up whatever I told her, deciding whether to believe me. But she gave that same look to her grandmother, too. Even at a very young age, Erica was a grave old soul and nobody's fool.

My mother probably would have tried to turn Tara and Ryan against me too, even though I was trying to be a super-mom when they were babies. She didn't get the chance. The Federal Marshals' from the Witness Protection whisked us away, and kept us hidden for nearly a year, keeping us all divided.

When we came back, I was different. The ironic thing was— so was she. She no longer had her youth or her health, and the son she'd idolized was so far gone by this time that even she had stopped making excuses for him. My father still adored her, but she had always discounted his love as of little value. Her grandchildren became her reason for living, and the year we were gone was rough on her. She had no one outside herself to fix. She was ready to overlook my inadequacies as a mother, in return for a role in her grandchildren's lives.

When we returned to the Bay area, my parents (my mother, really) offered to have all four of us move in with them temporarily, until I got on my feet. I was grateful, especially since none of us had an idea what "temporarily" might mean. After all, they had never seen me stand on my own feet before. They probably figured I didn't have any feet, and could even revert to lying on my back instead.

But I surprised her. In fact, I think I awed her. She saw me truly parenting my three children, supervising every aspect of their lives, shouldering all the responsibility for their well-being, putting their needs before my own. Slowly, she began to respect me. We experienced a season of mutual forgiveness, as we began to understand each other's wounds. Through our love for my children, we became friends, and then more than friends. We became mother and daughter at last.

I make it sound so easy and swift, but it wasn't. After all, here was a flamboyant, tactless woman, who evoked Gypsy Rose Lee or Lucille Ball, and a street-smart, tough ex-hooker who had already taken all the shit she was going to take. It was an explosive combination, and there were some dramatic scenes as we worked through our past on the way to our new friendship.

One of the most dramatic, and also one of the most healing, moments came when I finally convinced my mother to tell me the truth about my birth. Well, at least some of the truth.

In the past, my mother had used her secret knowledge about my parentage as a lever of control over me. Teasing hints (maybe you're French…or Greek) cloaked in hurt feelings and jealousy (why do you want another mother? I've done everything for you…I didn't have to have you) kept me on her leash. But now the power had shifted. I controlled her access to the grandchildren she loved; I could take them away from her at any time, and we both knew it.

So when I demanded, in the midst of a screaming argument about something totally different, that she had to pony up and let me know where I came from and stop withholding the truth from me, she finally caved. She spit a woman's name at me and told me to call her.

At first that's all she'd tell me, a name, a stranger who supposedly could tell me "something." But little by little, details trickled out. The name belonged to my half-sister's grandmother, who had helped arrange my adoption.

My mother had actually met my birth mother, before I was born. My birth mother came into my mother's photography studio to get portraits done of her seven-year-old daughter. She was pregnant and when my mother congratulated her on her condition, my birth mother confessed that she wasn't happy about it. She had recently married her second husband, who had four teenagers of his own, and they were trying to blend their families together. It was not going well. Another child wasn't in their plans.

That a total stranger would break down and tell my mother such intimate details didn't surprise me. People were always doing that with her. It also didn't surprise me that my mother went right to work finding a solution for her pregnant customer. Her solution was to adopt the baby herself. She got help with the paperwork from my birth mother's mother-in-law. Mom was vague on the specifics, and I suspect it was all somewhat under the table. "I just picked you up at the hospital," she said, "and then you were mine."

She still had the name and phone number of the grandmother. I don't know why she kept it; maybe she thought I'd want it later, or maybe she thought it would increase her hold over me. Either way, I'm glad she did.

When she finally told me the truth, something broken inside me healed. I started the process of finding my birth mother—it took years—but at the same time I accepted the mother who raised me as my only real mother. I recognized now that it wasn't just control that had caused her to withhold the truth for so long—it was also fear that I would reject her and replace her with someone else. I began to notice similarities between us that I had previously been too angry to see—for one thing, that word "unforgettable" applied to both of us. The truth allowed me to forgive her and find the love that had been there all along.

Our friendship took another step forward when the kids and I went back to live with Duke after he got out of prison. I didn't go back to him because I loved him; I went because I wanted my kids to have a father, like normal kids did. My mother strongly disagreed with my decision, especially because she would miss the kids. But this time she didn't try to fight me; she didn't threaten or belittle me. Instead she supported and trusted me, even helped me move. And when the relationship with Duke instantly started unraveling, she never once said "I told you so."

We got into the habit of seeing each other nearly every week. We'd go out to lunch just the two of us, and we'd talk about the kids and life in general. Or I'd drive over to pick her up and take her back to my place, so she could have time with the kids. One day after driving her home from spending the day at my house, I pulled into her driveway and turned to her. "I'm so grateful that you've been here for me," I said. "I don't know what I'd do without you."

She smiled at me as she got out of the car. Then she bent down and stuck her head back in the window. "You would do just fine," she said.

Two days later, she had her final stroke.

My father called to tell me she was in the hospital, alive, but just barely. He was crying on the phone. As I rushed to the hospital, all I could think was, "Not now, not now, I can't lose her now—not when I finally found her." As I drove through the tollbooth on the Golden Gate Bridge, I looked into the clouds, felt heaven stir and instinctively knew she was there.

At the hospital I learned that my father had just given the okay to take her off life support. I had a complete meltdown. I didn't just cry; I screamed at him, at the nurses, at everyone. I begged them to put her back on life support, swearing that I'd take care of her, feed her, clean her, do everything for her. I was in full fight-mode, ready to battle for my mother's life.

My father couldn't take it. He left her hospital room, where this scene was taking place, and I could hear him sobbing in the corridor outside. I took my mother's hand. She gripped mine in return. She squeezed it hard, again and again. Electrified, I tore out of the room to my father, saying "She's still here, she's gripping my hand, don't let her go!" But a nurse told me muscle spasms were common in dying people; they were letting go of themselves. I stared at her, not wanting to believe her.

The nurse was right. Just a few minutes later, my mother died. But she didn't die alone, because I was there with her. My mother really was unforgettable. I know this to be true because I will never forget her.

Reflections

So often, we seek from others what we crave inside ourselves. We long for others to love and approve of us so we can feel the love we can't seem to feel for ourselves.

We readily see our value in someone else's eyes when they accept us, give us affirmation or reassure us we're okay. While this quick fix may seem nourishing, it doesn't last because it comes from outside us. When we learn to feed ourselves from within, to drink from our own personal well of goodness, then we can truly begin to provide sustenance for ourselves.

This is easy to say, but not so easy to do. We want something or someone outside to tell us how good we are. We want material things that symbolize how good we've been. This belief feeds on itself, and creates a self-perpetuating cycle of need. You look outside yourself for validation, yet each response you get reinforces what you lack. You work harder; seek that validation more hungrily, and the more you find, the more dependent you become on it. Yet the emptiness within remains.

When my mother, who had always been my most severe critic, began to love and approve of me, it was because I had finally begun to approve of myself. Ironically, when I received her longed-for approval, I realized I had never needed it. Self-approval came first-I had it backward all along!

I could be angry that my mother was taken away just as we were beginning to know and love each other. Or I could be grateful that we found each other before she was taken away, and

> *that opportunity was lost forever. Which will give me the most peace? It's my choice.*

QUESTIONS:

1) Think of how you are your harshest critic. Name the aspects of yourself that most embarrass or shame you. Are those "unflattering" traits what other people in your life notice and criticize?

_____

_____

_____

2) Now, think of all of those likeable aspects of your personality and how others approve and compliment those good qualities.

_____

_____

_____

3) Do an experiment for the next month: explore, embrace and accept one of your so-called unattractive qualities, as best as you can manage. Prepare to watch the world around you have more compassion towards this part of you as well. Journal about the experiences that result.

_____

_____

_____

CHAPTER NINE

HOW ABOUT A RECEPTIONIST?

*When in doubt, look in the mirror and say: I believe in you.
Do this over and over, again and again. Change will come.*

What does a 25-year-old mother of three young children do when it's time to turn her life around? This was the question confronting me when I finally decided that a life of dishonoring myself was not going to cut it. Something had to shift.

I took a hard look at my situation. It wasn't encouraging. For the kids' sake, as well as my own, I had to leave Duke. My mother was dead, and my relationship with my father was the same as it always was—non-existent. Three innocent beings depended on me to give them the chance at a good life, and here I was with no skills, training or knowledge of how to make an honest living. I would not go backwards. I was weary to the bone, but I would not risk destroying my budding soul, or drag my children into anything that would impede their growth or sense of security.

Somehow I had to get a job. The problem was, there wasn't much I knew how to do. I had dropped out of school in seventh grade, dismissing education as trivial in all my teenaged wisdom. My work experience was in a field you can't put on your resume. My options looked bleak. Honestly, I was terrified.

I had to go back to school. I would have to be vulnerable and show up in a way I'd never shown up before—humble. I'd have to expose my ignorance. I could calculate simple arithmetic, but algebra? I had been to Saudi Arabia and Japan, but geography? Oh my god. To say I felt intimidated is an understatement. But I didn't see any other choice.

I made a promise to myself and set a goal. I vowed that by the age of forty I would no longer be struggling to survive. I accepted that the next fifteen years would be a period of necessary self-sacrifice; perhaps a type of absolution for the mistakes of the past. I worked very hard to accept, and not fight, the position I was in. I finally understood that my poor choices, impulsive behavior, lack of self-regard, and taste for the thrill that came with living in the face of danger, had created this destiny for myself. And if I created one destiny, I could create another.

So using the fuel that once enabled me to leave Gene—disciplined focus and raw courage—I propelled myself into the task of becoming an upstanding member of society.

My first step was getting my GED, in order to get into college and train for something that would support my family of four. The local community college gave the GED test, so I just went down and took it. I didn't study for it—for one thing, I wouldn't have known what to study. What do you learn in high school anyway? Also, there was no way I could study at home with three small children underfoot.

Luckily I was born with an aptitude for quick learning, and God knows I had plenty of street smarts,—together they must have made up for my lack of formal education. The tests took all day, and for half that, I was winging it, but I passed. I have no idea what my score was, and frankly, I didn't care. All I wanted was to pass so I could enroll in junior college.

I started my college career at Marin Community College in the early 1980s. To qualify for student loans I had to be on AFDC. I got a work-study grant that paid $980 a month for the four of us. I was able to earn a modest extra income by working evenings at the college. We got by, barely.

That first year passed in a sleep-deprived blur. Going to class, doing the assignments, caring for my kids, and working part-time doesn't leave much time for sleep, much less any kind of adult interaction. Don't ask me what I studied, because I don't remember. However I do recall being drawn to a General Education course in the study of religions. Here, again, was God in so many forms, but always with a similar message: You are love, and light is within. Of course, I didn't have the luxury of learning to enrich my knowledge base or understanding. I needed to learn a skill that would allow me to support my children.

My career aspirations at this point were severely practical. I had completed enough business courses to know I had what it took to be—a receptionist. I had the skills to greet people as they came in the door. I could candidly talk about almost anything and I genuinely enjoyed people. Up to now, my entertaining personality had been the only "skill set" I could rely on, but was this enough to serve as an asset in the marketplace. Now I needed a certificate saying I worked through educational courses to get here.

That year, I began having panic attacks. I'd be working on an assignment, or dealing with one of my children—just ordinary stuff—and suddenly my chest would feel tight and it was hard to breathe. Sometimes I'd get a cramping pain, like someone squeezing a hand around my heart. The doctor found nothing wrong with me, told me it was "all in my mind."

You might think panic attacks would have struck when I was living on the edge, but that's not how they work. When you are pumped up with adrenaline born from constant terror, you don't panic because you survive by telling yourself you can do anything. It's kind of like assuming a guise of grandiosity. Once the performance is over, you are left vulnerable with yourself—fears and all. Janis Joplin, who was actually very shy, once said that the only way she could get up on stage was by hyperventilating to the point of being stunned. Then she'd go out and wow everyone. After the act emptiness filled her and so did fear. That's what living on the edge is like. It is in the adrenaline that you soar.

But now, being law-abiding, conforming, and most of all human, made me vulnerable. I had to deal with life as it really was, without the game. I was afraid I couldn't do it because I didn't know how to be afraid. Fear was something I did not allow for or of myself. I only knew how to survive by stomping it out rather than looking it dead on—in the face.

Despite the challenges of little money, three children, and periodic panic attacks, I worked my butt off at college—what else could I do? In my second year, I took a job working in the college chancellor's office as a part-time receptionist. On the job training, I figured. I had an entertaining line of patter, and I wasn't afraid to approach people to see what they needed. I knew how to be adaptable and resourceful.

The office was a busy place, and soon I got to know many of the college faculty and staff. Some of them took an interest in me. One was Maria, a Brazilian woman who did career counseling and who was not impressed by my ambition to become a receptionist. She thought I should aim a little higher. I thought she was refined. She had style and a warm manner yet she told you like it was. Maybe she was a little bit pushy, but then, I always liked people who had a strong sense of self. She kept asking me to think about my future career, and I started to think maybe I could aim a little higher than a receptionist.

When I was close to getting my Associate's degree, which was all I needed to be a receptionist or administrate assistant, I began thinking about transferring to a four-year college. My priorities hadn't changed—what I did was less important than what I earned and the benefits I needed for my kids. But now I thought I might be able to find a higher-paying career. However, I still had no idea what my abilities were, or what I could do. So I went to Maria, who sat me down and gave me a battery of aptitude tests.

When she told me the tests showed I had the aptitude to be an attorney, I nearly choked. What was she thinking? I didn't have the option to dream—I needed a job—now! Becoming an attorney took time I just didn't have.

"Okay," she said, "then how about law enforcement?" At first, that seemed even more amusing, but as Maria talked about the opportunities, I stopped reacting and started listening. After all, I did know something about how law enforcement worked—just from the other side. Of course Maria didn't know that—no one at the college knew anything about my past. When Maria said I had the right stuff to be a Probation Officer, I nearly blurted out, "Oh my God, my old PO Barbara used to say that."

Maybe it was the irony, but that's when I knew I had found the right track. When I did call Barbara (my former P.O.) a few days later to tell her about my new career path, she laughed with both amusement and certainty. Then she told me I would be great.

Reflections

Today, I see the difference between the external struggle to survive and the internal struggle to grow. The external struggle is manifested by the attempt to manage the "things" within our environment—daily tasks, financial responsibilities, and social expectations.

The internal struggle mines our experiences, both negative and positive, for opportunities to learn and grow. A very real part of me wants no part in any further struggles at all. There is still a little girl lurking within me who wants to be rescued from the pain associated with living. Previously, when I would wonder, "What is the purpose of life?" my first response would be disappointment. I can easily call forth the pain I've endured, and sometimes forget the growth that came from it.

Maybe if someone had told me, "Acknowledge the fear and the pain; accept and release them, and you will receive the gifts of strength, knowledge, or courage," perhaps I would have approached my life with more confidence, stamina and openness. Even today, though, knowing what I know, doubt can return like a boomerang. Maybe I will never be free of it. But now I have the antidote— I know how to talk to myself, even in the face of disappointment. I think of all the times I stood in front of my mirror and said aloud, "I believe in you," even when I didn't. And you know what? The words worked. I changed.

QUESTIONS:

1) What do you tell yourself when you are disappointed in life and struggling either internally or externally? Does your internal dialogue make you feel good or lousy?

_____

_____

_____

_____

2) When you have difficulties, can you write a positive script for yourself of what you would like to hear to make yourself feel better?

_____

_____

_____

3) Can you write about what you need to learn when you are internally struggling about what to do next? Is it Faith? Forgiveness? Courage? Resiliance? All of the above?

_____

_____

_____

_____

4) In your current situation, imagine the outcome if you act with each of these characteristics?

_____

_____

_____

5) What action could you take to alleviate resentment from the past? For example, if you forgave a long-standing grievance with your ex, would you be open to a friendly relationship with a new man or woman?

_____

_____

_____

_____

_____

_____

6) What could happen next?

_____

_____

_____

_____

CHAPTER TEN

IRONY IS ALIVE AND WELL

*As you cross the bridge to accomplishment,
tenacity will strengthen your belief in your goal.*

It was hard for me to believe that I could actually achieve a career in law enforcement. Sometimes I thought I could—maybe—but more often I thought pursuing such an absurd dream would be a waste of time, effort and money. I remembered all the people I'd met along the way who I hoped would believe in me and would offer a lifeline that never came. Then I would think, maybe, just maybe, I could offer it to someone else.

In spite of my internal doubts, I let Maria guide me toward taking the required courses. While I was still getting my four-year degree, I applied for an entry-level position in the Marin County Probation Department. I was like an elated youngster on Christmas morning when the department called to offer me a job. Other people—normal people who knew what they were doing—thought I could do this. And that's when I started to genuinely believe that becoming a law enforcement professional wasn't such an absurdity after all.

It might not have been absurd, but it definitely was ironic. My first assignment within the Probation Department was as a group counselor at the Juvenile Hall. That was where everyone started, where you had to do your time before you could be promoted to Probation or Parole Officer. A counselor was not a deputized position. Group counseling at Juvenile Hall served both as a training ground and as a place to weed out those who weren't cut out to do this kind of work.

It became obvious fairly fast that I was well suited for the position. I had compassion for those kids because I, myself, had been in their place not so long ago. I wasn't in the least bit intimidated by their tactics, and I didn't buy their excuses or accept any lies. In other words, I wasn't soft; I was tough. I knew what could happen to these kids if they didn't get their act together fast, so I didn't waste my time, or theirs. I had worked so hard to grow from my experiences, and I was grateful to have the opportunity to share what I had learned. I suppose my desire was like a recovering alcoholic, sponsoring newcomers in the AA program.

Entering that career was the beginning of redemption for me. It was an opportunity to give something back from a place I knew. Redemption helped me build a platform where I could do some work on my soul as well.

At Juvenile Hall, I was very different than the other counselors. Many of them just marked their time there, waiting to work up the ladder in the department. Many worked second shift—3 p.m. to 11 p.m.—or the graveyard shift as a second job just to augment their income. But for me it was much more. I saw my role as important to those kids, and when I walked through those doors, I was fully present.

It's not that the other counselors didn't care about the kids at all—many cared deeply. But their focus was always on the past, and they joined the kids in making excuses for their bad behavior, their poor parenting, their poverty, their neighborhoods. Nobody ever gave the kids a plan on how to change. They didn't believe the kids even had the power to change their lives.

I really took exception to that. I told the kids they were choosing to damage their own lives and until they realized that the consequences were real and painful, their choice would remain uninterrupted as well as their consequences.

I could talk to the kids from a street level. Kids at Juvenile Hall didn't give a damn who you were. They had no respect for authority. I'd come in to work, and some girl would come up to me and say something like, "Bitch, you think you're cute wearing your tight-ass jeans. You ain't nothing to me." They insulted the counselors, trying to put our backs against the wall to see what we were made of.

Most counselors would do one of two things. Female counselors would often try to massage the anger down, try to sympathize with the anger, saying "I know you're angry, but you don't have to say that." Male counselors would be more likely to try penalties, like "I'm gonna put you on lock down till you clean your mouth."

I didn't do either. When a kid mouthed off, I'd raise my eyebrows and say, "Is that the best you can do? Is that all you've got?" They'd look surprised and reply, "Say What?"

The other counselors, and the system as a whole, focused too much on placing blame somewhere—on the kids themselves, their parents, the environment they came from. I wasn't looking for someone or something to blame. The truth, to me, was that each kid was responsible for their own behavior. They were in charge of their own lives. And if we showed them the tools they needed, they could learn to change if they elected to.

It took me a long time to learn that truth. I just wanted to save those kids some time. Sometimes I was successful, sometimes not, but I was there to give something different a chance. They say something needs to change in order to become different; my goal was to try something different, and that is what I did.

One thing I remembered from my own stays in Juvie was how leaders emerged among the kids, and how those leaders could reinforce dysfunctional behavior. The tribal posture strengthens each member's stance. I pulled the leaders away from their acolytes, defusing their power, and I used those opportunities to talk to them one-on-one. Once, after dinner, I was in the kitchen with a group of kids, supervising them as they cleaned up. One of the leaders held forth there, a boy about 15 or 16 years old, bragging how he'd convinced a much younger girl at his school to perform a sex act on him in the boys' bathroom. I cut him off before he could finish his story, handed him a mop and dragged him into the dining room. When it was just the two of us, cleaning under the tables, I confronted him.

"How did that really happen?" I asked him. "Because if it did, you deserve consequences for that. It's a violation, and I want you to tell me why and how it is wrong."

He backpedaled pretty quickly, saying he'd made it all up. We talked for awhile about why he felt he needed to get "his respect" from such a tale of conquest. He opened up about the put-downs he had experienced from his peers—this would let them know what he was a capable of. We spoke about how poisonous lies can be harmful—towards everyone. And we talked about reaping what you sow.

With one simple act of heartfelt understanding, the potentially poisonous virus was shut down—before it could infect all the kids on the unit. With one boy acting out—then owning his own actions, and connecting to his heart—all was diffused.

I spent my years at Juvenile Hall lobbying for programs that taught the kids personal responsibility. By the time I left, we had sex education classes that talked about AIDS and condoms; calisthenics classes that taught about physical health and body issues; programs about creating healthy relationships.

My colleagues weren't always happy about these programs. It meant more work for them. They couldn't just sit behind a partition and wait for some kid to act out. They had to do more than just warehouse and baby sit these kids.

Implementing those classes, and my little successes at work, those things made me feel vindicated. And they affirmed my decisions to change my life.

Of course, vindication and affirmation were never my goals. I went back to school so I could get a good job. I got a good job so I could pay the bills, support my kids, and get us all health benefits. By achieving a position with the Probation Department, I achieved those goals, and that was a solid start. But even greater, my new position gave me a chance to redeem the past. It also illustrated that each of us has an impact on one another as to how our paths intersect—we have a choice to cross the road or connect with one anther along our journey.

That was the beginning of redemption for me, taking that job at Juvenile Hall. It was an opportunity to give something back from a place I knew. Redemption helped me build a platform where I would do some serious work on my soul.

Between raising my children and working swing shifts at Juvenile Hall, I continued my education, now setting my sights on obtaining my 4 year degree. Now, I not only had a vague hope for a brighter future, I had out-and-out dreams and a dream that no longer seemed absurd. They were realistic, if I was willing to do the work. I knew

I was in the right field, and I wanted to become first a Probation Officer, and then work my way up the ladder in the department.

I achieved the first step of becoming a Probation Officer in 1987, right after I received my Bachelor's degree, three years after I had started at Juvenile Hall as a group counselor. I now worked with adults, not juveniles. I was even more passionate about my work.

Again, my peers and supervisors considered me "different" and—that word again—"unforgettable." They sometimes also called me a "Maverick" because, although I knew the rules and abided by them, I was not motivated by them. I sought new ways to make the rules work to the advantage of the court, the victims, and my probationers. My job evaluations were always sterling, the box "exceeds expectations" regularly checked. My superiors gave me difficult cases because they started to believe I could handle just about anything. My coworkers considered me somewhat of a mystery because no one could figure out how I knew the things I knew. That's because no one—not one person—knew about my past. As far as I was concerned, it was going to stay that way. My past was dead. The only things left were the lessons I'd learned that could help me do my job, and the intuitive understanding I brought to the sad, angry, and defeated people who showed up on my case load.

I was no miracle worker. This was not a movie, where the ex-hooker-with-a-heart-of-gold saves young girls from a life of prostitution. I didn't try to connect with clients through our shared suffering. They didn't need someone to stand by their side; they needed someone to show them the way out. That meant they needed to be told the truth, even when the truth wasn't pretty. Whether they accepted the truth or acted upon it was up to them.

There's a difference between tolerance and understanding. Early on, I worked with a probationer named Dwight, who I quickly realized had the potential and internal strength to become a success at anything he chose. A former athlete, Dwight played college football and was talented enough to be drafted into the NFL, but an injury brought his dreams of a football career to an abrupt end. Worse, he suffered severe pain, which his doctors managed by prescribing opiates.

The injury healed, but his need for morphine did not. Within a year Dwight started injecting heroin and committing burglaries to support his addiction.

When Dwight landed on my caseload, the first thing I told him was that I would absolutely not tolerate his out-of-control criminal behavior. But I understood the circumstances that got him into this dangerous place in his life. I empathized with his broken dreams. He was bright and capable of making a new start, plus he had a wife and small child dependent on him to salvage the remnants of his life. My understanding, I knew, would not help Dwight nearly as much as holding him accountable for his behavior. Something that he was unable to do for himself in this fractured state.

He struggled with his addiction, making some progress and then falling back. I would call him to come in for random drug testing, knowing all the while he was using. When the tests came back positive, I didn't let him slide. I violated him, took him to court, and he was sent back to jail. The judge ordered him to complete a drug treatment program. Again, with enormous strength and conviction, he pulled himself back from the brink. When he completed the program, I attended his graduation with much satisfaction. I met his wife and child, and they, too, were proud of him.

Dwight's story does not have a happy ending. Ultimately, he could not cope with the pain and disappointment life had thrown at him. He went back to using, and his hard-won gains disappeared. He was disgusted by the man he saw in the mirror each morning—just another criminal and addict who would leave a legacy of pain and loss behind him. Less than a year after his recovery graduation, Dwight shot his last bag of dope in a darkened Safeway parking lot, and died of an overdose.

I probably remember Dwight so well because I was unable to help him alter his life pattern. My compassion, my efforts to hold him accountable for his actions, could not make him see the choices, they could not save him from the despair he felt for himself. Dwight's story underlined the lesson I had learned the hard way: our success or failure is up to us. Our choices are our own—as are our successes and failures.

I could be responsible for just one person's success—mine. For others, all I could do was shine a light down the path and offer up the a help line called hope. It is for each person to grab hold and choose a new direction.

Reflections

Balance is key to constructing a full life. Engagement in the world is necessary, but so is the growth of the soul.

When we are young, we're given some instruction in how to form strategies for worldly success. Think of when we go to the gym. Our goal is to build muscle. We accept the fact that we are going to sweat, ache, and spend a lot of time doing something difficult. Once we see the muscles developing, we are encouraged to continue sweating and aching. (This is why there are mirrors all over gyms.) We see it, we do it, and we can easily measure the results.

Yet in our souls' evolution, there is no such measurement. So how do you know when you're making progress? An enlightened person might tell you it's through acceptance and tranquility that you begin to see the benefits of the journey. For me this is a bit esoteric. If I am going to the "gym of life," paying my dues, spending my time, and working my muscles, I want results I can measure and touch.

I believe this is true of many people, heck, maybe even everyone. But I know that when I am pursuing a goal which I can measure by results, I am no longer simply being in the moment, which is my soul's ultimate goal—being, not doing.

I believe that setting goals and working hard to achieve them is the way to live a happy and productive life. I also believe that accepting what is, not what could be, is the way to live a happy and productive life. Can both beliefs be true? I think they can. It's called a paradox.

QUESTIONS:

1) Have you ever pursued an absurd dream, thinking you are wasting time, effort, and money, but your gut says do it anyway?? What was the dream? Do you still want it? What was/is the outcome of following your dream? Who were/are your lifelines along the way?

_____

_____

_____

_____

_____

2) Is it possible to enjoy the journey toward your goals? Can you take fulfillment in the small steps along the way?

_____

_____

_____

_____

3) What has been the blessing in not quickly getting what you wanted?

_____

_____

_____

CHAPTER ELEVEN

REAL SEXUAL LIBERATION

Liberation is the freedom to be your dreams.

I was now a college graduate, working in a career I loved, and supporting my three kids; how could I ask for more? I knew I was lucky to have gotten this far, but I did ask for more. Why shouldn't I have a real relationship with a man, one who didn't degrade me?

I don't think I really expected it to happen though. I now had girlfriends and work friends, and I tried to let this be enough. I had a social life in spite of the demands of three small children. Several other single moms and I befriended and supported each other, and we rotated our kids from one house to the other so every Saturday somebody could go out and have a reprieve. We'd go out with each other to Marin County night spots, dance and have a few drinks, laugh a lot.

Sometimes I met a guy I liked enough to date a few times, but I never let them near my children. They were always in their thirties, wore tailored suits, had good jobs. In the early 1980s there were several hot spots, especially in upscale Marin County. I was in my mid-twenties and good looking, and of course, I excelled at flirtation. If I wanted a date, I could get one.

But that's all it was—dating. I never let anyone get closer than that. I hadn't had sex since I left Duke, when Ryan was almost two. By this time he was almost four.

One Saturday night, a girlfriend and I went to a popular club in a woodsy location adjacent to the home of George Lucas. Despite its trendy reputation and live music, it wasn't an upscale place—it seemed to be frequented by old hippies. When we walked in I took a look around and said, "There is nobody even clean in here!" To me, "clean" meant not only that someone showered regularly, but that they were well groomed and well dressed. For years, I wore mink coats and high heels every day, and as a single working mom had only recently relaxed my dress code to slacks and sweaters. I'd finally started wearing blue jeans a year earlier, but only rarely.

My girlfriend and I sat at the bar, and she grabbed a guy she knew as he walked past us, saying "At least this one is clean." His name was Clark and yeah, he was clean, although he was wearing jeans. At first I thought, "Whatever," because he wasn't my type at all. He was sweet and boyish—he was 22 to my 27—and maybe just a bit too cute. His red hair made him look even younger, and kind of naïve. If it had been five years earlier, I would have quickly dismissed him as a square.

Things were different now. I had suffered enough degradation and grief to know not to scoff at decency and kindness, and Clark's charm grew on me quickly. He asked me out, and I said yes.

We hit it off. Our dates were always fun, and we laughed a lot. But we shared our sorry stories from our past too. Like me, Clark came from an upper-middle class family that was broken and totally empty. His mother was an alcoholic; his wealthy professional father left his family to run off with his secretary. Clark's baby sister drowned because no one was watching her; their mother was too drunk to pay attention to her five children wandering around alone in a 2,500-square-foot house with a pool. Shortly after his sister's death, his mother died. His father and the new wife, not wanting to be saddled with the four remaining children, sent Clark and his three older brothers away to military boarding school. Clark was six when he was shipped off for literally being a red-headed stepchild.

Naturally, with an empty, loveless childhood behind him, Clark graduated into a rebellious teenager who partied and got into trouble. We identified strongly with each other, both of us little black sheep who needed to be loved. I shared some of my childhood stories with him too, although I stopped short of telling him I'd literally made a living on the street.

What I had that he didn't was a family, the one I'd made myself. Clark wanted a family very badly, some place that he belonged, and I wanted my kids, especially my son, to have a father. Each of us had what the other yearned for, we fit, and it wasn't long before I tumbled headlong into the first true love affair of my life.

I think the first time I realized how much I loved Clark was when he built Ryan a workbench. Clark was a handy guy; he worked as a plumbing contractor, and was an excellent amateur carpenter. On our first Christmas together, when we hadn't been dating very long, he made a child-sized workbench for Ryan complete with all the right holes to hold screwdrivers and nails and stuff like that. Ryan was all boy, and when he saw that workbench his eyes lit up. He thought Clark was magic. I thought Clark was magic.

He was magic in bed too, although it took me a while to find this out. I wouldn't sleep with him right away, because the wall I'd put up to protect myself was a strong one. I knew how sex can make you vulnerable, and I didn't want to risk the security I had worked so hard to achieve. But after a month of dating (which in the 1980s was a long time), I began to remove a few bricks from my wall. I thought that I'd let him have a chance with me, and we had sex.

Except we didn't "have sex." Instead we made love, which was an alien concept to me. I had never made love before, and I had no idea how to do it. I know this sounds odd considering my past, but it's true. One of the first times we had sex, Clark put his hand on my neck to pull me closer to him. I immediately reacted by kicking him in the chest, throwing him off me. He said, "What the hell?" He looked so bewildered, but I didn't see that right away.

"You grabbed my neck," I said. "What do you think you're doing?" I was furious—and scared.

"I was just trying to touch your face," he said, "I was loving you."

I thought he was trying to choke me.

Kindness, soft touches, cherishing—these had all been absent from my sex life before. I never permitted a man to kiss me, or look into my eyes. Before Clark I didn't know what real sex was, because real sex includes love.

That incident wouldn't be the last time (in the bedroom and outside of it) that I had trouble letting my guard down, showing Clark my vulnerabilities. It didn't happen overnight, but through our relationship, slowly, I learned. I knew I had found a life partner, and was no longer alone.

We moved in together in late 1986, and about six months later we got married. I chose April 19th as our wedding date, because it was my mother's birthday and I so wished she was alive to share this day with me. It also happened to be Easter Sunday. Everybody said I couldn't get married on Easter, but I did. Partly because as soon as you tell me I can't do something, I'll try like hell to do it, but also because I thought Easter was a perfect time for our wedding. Easter is all about rebirth, and I felt as if I was being reborn. Easter is also about forgiveness, and I was forgiving the past by starting a new future.

We didn't have much money for a fancy wedding. I think we had about $1,200 to our name—and that was both of us put together. I bought my wedding gown at Goodwill, and we held the ceremony and reception at McNears Park in San Rafael. The kids walked down the aisle with me. On the invitations we asked everyone to bring something to share. It was a potluck wedding. It was great.

I loved married life. For the first time, I experienced the bond of a family. It was like sleeping in a comfortable bed of your own after years of toughing it out on the neighbor's couch. Clark adopted my kids, and the youngest two, Tara and Ryan, took his name. We sat down to dinner together every night and engaged in conversation. We shared the trivialities of domestic tasks. We played with the kids—Clark really loved to play with the kids. Maybe it made up for never having anyone play with him when he was a kid. On the other hand, having been brought up in military school, he liked order, so he was a strict disciplinarian. This was great for me, since it meant I no longer had to be the only one setting and maintaining the rules. Sometimes I could relax and have fun, too.

We scrimped and saved to send the kids to parochial school, even though neither of us was Catholic. We wanted them to have structure, and since we were both working fifty hours a week, their school took up some of the slack. We still found time to be involved—we went to PTA meetings, Clark did some basketball coaching, I helped with rummage sales. We were truly living the life I had always wanted, the life I'd seen on television sitcoms when I was a child, the life I pretended to have when I lived with Duke. Only now it was real.

For the first year of our marriage, we lived in a rental house, but then we took the plunge and bought a home of our own. It was a fixer-upper that we busted our butts renovating, but it was ours. To my vast surprise, my father lent us the money for the down payment. He had been slowly (and I mean really slowly) warming up to me as he watched me go through college and succeed at my job. When I married Clark, I think he started to believe I was actually going to make it.

My relationship with my father grew even stronger when I became pregnant with the child both Clark and I wanted badly. I was thrilled to be having a baby with the man I loved, but it was a difficult pregnancy. For the last six months, I had to go to the University of California Medical Center for monitoring every week. My father lived just down the street from the clinic, so I started taking him out to lunch after my check ups. Our regular lunches, his finally seeing me as a success, these things gave us a platform on which to build a relationship. He was never going to be a warm man, but we became friends. He began to come to our home for all our family gatherings. He remained a hands-off grandfather, but he was there.

My life sounds idyllic, doesn't it? In many ways it was, but it was so different from anything I'd known before that adjusting to happiness was not easy. Shortly after our daughter Gina was born in 1987, my panic attacks, which I thought were gone, came back. When Gina was still a baby, Clark and I took the four kids to a Kinderphoto at the mall for a family portrait. It was chaos, coordinating smiles and holding the kids' attention as we posed for the photos. Even the photographer could see that although we were a lot, we were a happy family.

When the photos were ready to pick up, I went to the Kinderphoto on my lunch hour to get them. The sales lady spread the photos out on the counter for me, and I looked down at this bunch of happy, smiling people, two adults in love, and four kids eager for life. I had to ask the lady for a chair so I could sit down. My heart was beating so hard it hurt, and I had trouble breathing. All I could think was, "I have to be there completely for all these people."

I was in this for the long haul—not just for a play or two, but for the whole game. What if I couldn't do it? What would happen to the people I loved?

This time, I did not let my fear sabotage my happiness or build walls around my heart. I remembered to breathe, and I let the love in. My marriage thrived, and my kids did, too. When they became teenagers, of course they pushed our buttons, because that's what teenagers do, but Clark and I were tough, and above all, we stood in solidarity together. We seldom fought in front of them, and presented a unified front. I forgot that three of the kids weren't actually his. For a long time he forgot it too.

Tara and Ryan thought of Clark as their dad, and even Erica, who was nine when we got married, claimed him as her dad even though she hadn't changed her name to his. When she was in seventh grade, she turned in her homework that Clark had signed (the school required a parent to sign all homework). The teacher looked at the signature and said, "Clark Bonelli? I used to have a student named Clark Bonelli when I taught at Feather River School." Erica said, "That's my dad!"

The teacher looked at her. Not only is Erica black, but Clark is only twelve years older than her. "No, that's not your father," he said.

"It is my father!" she snapped back.

"Well, he can't be," stated the teacher, and moved on, although Erica continued to argue. It was pretty funny when Clark and I went to the school's open house that year, and the teacher recognized the grown up Clark who claimed Erica as his daughter.

The kids laugh about it now, but Clark and I were regimented. We allowed them to go out with friends and to parties once they were teenagers, but we enforced curfews. And, when they came home, I required them to come into our bedroom to say good night. I'd say, "Let me smell your hands, your hair and your breath." Then I'd tell them they were loved and kiss them goodnight. I smelled their hair for cigarette smoke, their hands for pot, and their breath for alcohol. I knew all the tricks, and very little got past me. Oh, they complained at the time, but home was a safe place where they knew the rules. They could trust it.

Eighty percent of what we earned went to their education. We paid for parochial school, flute lessons, seasonal ski trips, Boy Scouts—Ryan went to Ireland once with the Boy Scouts. Since we were in the lower financial echelon in Marin County, this wasn't easy. The kids' friends all came from families much more affluent than ours.

Yet our house was where kids liked to hang out. When we had birthday parties or sleepovers, which were nearly every weekend, there would be an additional two to a dozen kids in our house. We'd feed them with Pizza Hut pizzas, because it was all we could afford. Maybe our kids felt bad that we didn't have the big TVs or the backyard swimming pool, but if they did they didn't say so.

And when it came time to just be together, we had family movie night at our house nearly every Friday.

Our kids loved what we had, and they loved us. One Valentine's Day Clark and I went out to dinner, and when we came home we found that the kids had scattered rose petals from our backyard through the house, leading to our bedroom. They had the "Boyz II Men" CD playing, the one with The Perfect Long Song. They were all little rappers back then. Because Clark didn't drink (his family had some alcoholics), they had Martinelli's Sparkling Cider on ice, with two glasses, waiting for us.

It was so sweet, but to tell the truth, it was hard to have great, primal sex in a house full of kids and their friends. Somebody always wanted to come in the bedroom and watch TV with us. We had to make time to get away, so we could be together just the two of us. One year when we didn't have much money (nearly every year) so we went to a "Marriage Encounter" weekend sponsored by the Catholic Church. We thought we could save money because if you signed up for the Encounter you got a free room in the Dominican College dormitory.

At the Encounter we sat with a bunch of other couples in a big room and listened to all the terrible problems people had with their marriages. They all boiled down to the same thing—no one was talking to each other. When they did talk, they talked so politely you couldn't tell what they were saying. Everyone was taking themselves very seriously indeed. Except Clark and me—we kept glancing at each other and rolling our eyes. When would this be over so we could be alone?

That night when we got to our room it wasn't any better. First of all, there were twin beds, obviously made specifically for skinny nuns. The dormitory walls were so thin that you could hear a tiny fart from the next room, and the rooms were full of couples with marital problems, who were doing a lot more squabbling than farting. Clark looked at me and said, "We've got to get out of here."

And we did. The next morning we fibbed and told the staff that one of the kids was sick and we had to go home early. We went to the Bay Meadows racetrack and bet 2 to win place and show on the horses and laughed. That night we got a room at a Motel 6 along the highway and made as much noise as we wanted.

That's what our marriage was like for ten of the thirteen years we were together. It wasn't always easy, but we were able to make it work.

We made our divorce work too. The marriage ended, as all things do. Strange, but it ended because of something that should have brought us closer together.

In 1989, Clark was working as a plumbing contractor, spending a lot of time underneath houses and buildings, working on the pipes. When the Loma Prieta earthquake struck San Francisco that October, that's where Clark was, underneath a house. He and everyone who cared about him were terrified the building would collapse and bury him in rubble. He escaped safely, and immediately began thinking about a new career.

He thought he might try law enforcement—he knew a little about it being married to me. I encouraged him. I thought it would be cool because we could talk the same language. Plus we both knew what life was like on the other side of the street—personally I thought he'd be great.

It took him a few years to become a cop, because he had to keep working while attending the Police Academy—we had all those kids to support. But he finally became a full-fledged police officer when we'd been married about ten years. And that's when everything started to change.

With power, he became a completely different person, as so many do. He did what 80 percent of people do. He shut off. He stopped being accountable to anybody but his ego. One day he came home and announced to me, "I've never cheated on you, but I'm going to."

I'd committed myself fully to Clark; I had no intention of sleeping with anyone else, ever. And I was long, long finished with tolerating a relationship that would degrade me in any way. Earlier in our relationship, I told him that if he ever cheated on me, he'd better have the balls to walk out the door. He knew I meant it. So when he declared he was going to cheat, I told him "You need to go."

I didn't expect him to go, but he did and he never came back. As far as I know he didn't even look back. Neither I nor the kids ever fully understood it.

Disposable woman, that's me—the feeling that haunted me through my childhood returned. The man who promised to stand by me forever changed his mind, and I found myself alone once more. And Clark's departure hurt the kids, too. He was their father, after all.

I think at least 60 percent of the love I felt for Clark was based on how he was as my kids' dad. Maybe that's how I was able to forgive him and work with him to make the divorce as easy as possible on them. We used the same attorney. He paid child support for the only child he now claimed—the one he fathered.

The last thing Clark said to me as my husband was "You know more about me than I am willing to know about myself." It was cold comfort. But we learn what we need to learn, and then we must move on.

Reflections

They say that it is better to have loved and lost than never to have loved at all. I agree.

Love expands your heart. It offers you the chance to dream with another person, and it multiplies the opportunities for you to manifest those dreams. But it means it is no longer all about you—your needs, wants, or interests are no longer primary. You no longer set the course and drive alone.

The Bible says when two are brought together in my name, greater is the prayer. I say when two can place self interest second, and put the union's interests first, all interests will be served. This is faith.

We are like children in many ways. We place our self interests first because we are afraid that if we don't, no one will, and we won't lead the life we want. When you do that in a relationship, it means you've given up on faith that God or the relationship can provide for you. Instead, you are acting from fear and self interest. In faith, we move toward the unknown, toward what we cannot see. In faith, we reach the place we want to go.

The trick to getting what we all want is to move out of the way. In previous relationships, I had been the navigator and sometimes the pilot, and I ended up alone, unsure of how I got there. How could this be? I recognize it was the absence of faith that carried me to a state of being alone. Today I choose to be different…and so it is.

QUESTIONS:

1) Write down a broken dream, one you went for but didn't achieve, and how that experience lead you to create new intentions and new goals. Did you end up getting something better for you? Did something you didn't expect but needed even more for your soul's growth occur?

_____

_____

_____

_____

_____

_____

_____

_____

_____

_____

_____

_____

_____

_____

_____

_____

2) Oprah Winfrey says, "God can dream a bigger dream for you than you can ever dream. Real success comes when you learn to act as if everything depends on you and pray as if everything depends on God." What would your prayer to God be today?

CHAPTER TWELVE

THE PAST RETURNS

To remain honest in the face of conflict is true nobility.

Even when my marriage was strong and healthy, and I was raising my children, most of my time and a great deal of my energy went toward my work. I continued to love what I did, and my progress in the department was swift.

Maybe that was the problem; it was too swift. When I was working with my clients, counseling the people on my case load, I was on solid ground. I understood the pain and confusion my clients faced. I knew the games they played, and I knew how not to play with them. But among my colleagues and superiors in the department, the ground turned to shifting sand. When I paid attention to my colleagues, (which wasn't often), I felt I was sinking. I had moved from the primal level of survival to a calmer environment where people appeared to play nice, even if they didn't always say what they meant. I had more street smarts than most, but emotionally I was still ten to fifteen years behind everyone else. I didn't know the rules of the political games, and I had no idea how to handle manipulative office gossip. Small talk bored me, and I was never any good at diplomacy and tact; I saw it as a waste of time. Why not be direct and say what you mean?

I had never disclosed the events of my wayward past to anyone in the department—or anyone outside of it either, for that matter. I didn't consider that part of my life relevant to my new one. I wanted the shame to remain in the past. After all, my life on the street was well behind me for more than a decade.

But I was wrong. The past was relevant, as it was about to prove.

After Juvenile Hall, I got promoted to the adult probation department, where I prepared bail reports every morning. I'd go to the holding cells at the jail and in the police stations, and interview everyone who had been arrested the night before. I'd try to determine what, if any, ties they had to the community, whether they had jobs, family, a stable place to live, anything that would encourage them to stick around and show up for their trials. Then I'd go back to my office and check out everything they told me. I'd run the records, call their contacts and write up a mini-report for the judge, either recommending a bail increase or considering them for release on their own recognizance. I started at six a.m. and would interview anywhere from eight to twenty people, depending how many people the police arrested.

The people in the holding cells didn't present their best sides, that's for sure. Many were hung-over, and all of them stank. Most were men. I was attractive, and men had always responded to me—I wasn't the most beautiful woman around, but whatever it was I had, it worked for men. Except for the very beginning of my career on the street, I never had to approach men. They approached me. I made them nervous, but they liked me. My reaction was the opposite—they didn't make me nervous at all. I knew about them and understood them.

The chief of my division and I got along well, and he worried about me going into the holding cells, thinking I might not know how to handle these "tough" guys. They might try to give me a hard time! He'd waylay me before I went to the cells, warned me about whoever he thought might scare me then he gave me a pep talk and some advice on how to handle myself. "Don't let them give you any shit," he'd say. His macho protectiveness made me smile inside. Every day I worked in Juvenile Hall, someone called me "bitch." In the cells, the guys called me ma'am, trying to bullshit me. But I kept my amusement to myself. I knew how to handle the chief's type, too. I placated him with "Okay, thanks very much, Chief," immediately went on to do my business.

That was a mistake. I should have recognized the chief had an interest in how well I did my job as much as he had an interest in my looks. He would watch my skirt when I walked. But it wasn't just that—I did my job well, and the chief was excited that he had this hotshot newbie who would take on anything. I made his department look good. He sang my praises to his superiors, and I became known as a rising star in the department.

I continued to love my job, do it well, and grow professionally. The chief was proud of me, I got promoted regularly, and I was happy. But for all my street smarts and my college degree, I was still remarkably naïve in some ways.

I ignored the people who told me I was going too fast and making the job look too easy. "Take your time," they said. "You don't have to burn through all those files." But although I was proud of my advancements and needed the extra money, the promotions were not what motivated me. I simply loved the work. I was making a difference, and I knew it.

It took years before I became aware of the hostility brewing against me in the department. And when I was made aware, it came as a complete surprise.

I'm still not sure how it got started, though I suspect I received too much attention from the high echelons of power. It was the 1980s, and not too many women held management positions yet, so as I progressed up the ladder I was visible, and other women resented me. A thick stream of professional jealousy coursed through the department; for many of the people who worked there, anytime a little bit of malicious gossip came their way, they jumped on it.

I suspect Duke, my old mate and the biological father of two of my kids, lit the spark. He lived in Marin County then, and still smoked pot. He got pulled over a couple of times, and once he even left a note with the department receptionist for me, saying he wanted to talk. I never answered it—I was done with him, done with that life. But I knew he had some contact with the department, so it was possible that he was shooting off his mouth, saying something like, "She used to be a hooker!"

Once it was out, my colleagues made quick work of my past. They went to the Chief and told him. He sent someone to do some digging around, and they found my arrest record from the Juvenile Division in San Francisco, even an old mug shot, taken when I was 17, right after Gene had knocked out my teeth. It wasn't a pretty picture.

I knew nothing about this until one day when I was in court, presenting a case recommendation to the judge. A colleague pulled me out of court, saying the chief needed to talk to me right now. When you're pulled out of court to talk to the chief, it's a bad sign. I knew that, yet had no inkling of what was coming.

At the office, I walked into the conference room to find my direct supervisor, the chief, and the union representative waiting for me. The union guy really threw me—I almost asked him what he was doing here. Union reps only show up when it's serious. Then I saw the materials spread out on the conference table: arrest records, reports from my stays in Juvenile Hall, that mug shot. Everything, going all the way back to when I was 13.

They proceeded to lay into me. One of them pointed at my mug shot with disgust and called me a liar because I'd never come clean with them about my past. My chief's face was red, and the veins in his forehead visibly pulsed as he said he would never have hired me if he'd known. He didn't have people like me working for him. Unworthy people. Filthy people. Whores.

It was worse than being beaten by my pimp. Sitting there, I was totally unprotected and alone. I didn't live on high alert anymore—I thought danger was in the past, too. I thought I had become one of them, decent and law abiding. I earned a degree. I was married. I had four kids. I'd bought a house, paid taxes, attended the PTA. I had worked so hard to get out of the gutter and now, my coworkers told me the gutter was where I still belonged. The people turning on me were the very people I had aspired to be like—educated, taxpaying, upwardly mobile citizens, pillars of integrity and upholders of decency. These allegedly decent people no longer wanted me taking a seat at their table.

The chief put me on immediate leave pending formal litigation and termination. They weren't just going to punish me; they were going to get rid of me forever. Never mind my excellent evaluations for five consecutive years. Never mind my accomplishments with my cases. Never mind anything. Nothing about who I was now had any relevance in light of where I'd once been. Wow—I went into shock.

I don't remember how I escaped that conference room. I wasn't numb with shock; numb would have been easier. I was one big raw nerve, exposed to the outside air and humming with pain. But the worst was still to come. I had to go home. I had to tell my husband what had happened. I had to let my kids know our life, our security were at risk of being dismantled.

I had been so careful to never mention my past, to anyone.

When people asked me questions about my childhood or adolescence, I gave vague answers that revealed only that I had a difficult youth and ended up on the street. I never elaborated beyond that, and people did not ask. Even my dad, who knew I'd been on the street, didn't know any of the details. My kids knew I'd been a wild teenager, but had no idea what I meant by 'wild.' Not even Erica, who was old enough to remember some things, but not old enough to know what those things meant. If she or anyone else asked about her biological dad, I just passed it off as a youthful indiscretion, long past and forgotten.

And Clark, well, although I had mentioned to him that I'd spent some time in Juvenile Hall and on the streets, I never went into detail with much else —and he never asked. I don't think he wanted to know. That was fine with me because I didn't want him to see me from that light, either—not so much to protect me, but because I wanted to protect him from the hurt it would cause. I loved him so much.

Telling Clark was one of the hardest things I've ever done. I had to watch the expressions parade across his face: first, disbelief; then, confusion, hurt, anger; and finally, betrayal. Fear quickly overshadowed all of those emotions. We'd bought our house only a year before. We paid for our kids to go to parochial school. We were building a life together, and now all of it was endangered. At this time, I made more money than he did, and if I lost my job—and my whole career—we had nothing to replace it. We stood to lose everything we had worked for.

For the next month or so, while I was on leave and the department pursued its goal of firing me, I stayed at home and grieved. I had built a life I loved, and I was losing it. I could barely leave the house. I felt like I was wearing a big sign on my chest that said "Whore." What if I went to the grocery store and ran into a parent from my kids' school? I was a room mother and active in the school community—everyone knew me. Had they heard about my past, too? Would they shun me, call me names, treat me like dirt? When I did go out of the house, I often ended up just driving around, afraid to get out of the car. Sometimes I felt like crashing the car into a wall. I wanted to die.

I had shut down and given up, and I might have stayed that way for a long time, maybe forever, but a wonderful thing happened. It took me a while to hear him, but my father—the man who once called me a loser and a trollop and disowned me as his daughter, the man who said I contaminated his bathroom, the man who had never been there for me—stood up and fought for me. He got mad! My cautious, emotionally colorless father was outraged and wrote letters to the department and the county, demanding that I be reinstated. He railed against the judgmental idiots who couldn't see how far I had come and how I had succeeded against all odds. He scathingly reminded them that it was not legal, nor right, to punish adults for the mistakes they made as juveniles.

My father's anger woke me from my depression. I looked around and was amazed that it wasn't just my father who was standing up for me, either. Others who knew me, even those who had known me when I was an abandoned kid, like Nancy's mom, wrote letters. Professionals who knew me from my work at the Civic Center wrote letters testifying to my goodness and my competence. I was stunned.

And it made me shore up. I got angry—"those motherfuckers don't know who they're messing with," I thought. I went into street fight mode.

I used to tell inmates, "If you can take the bad stuff that's happened to you and use it to light a fire under you that mobilizes you to act, you will become your greatest asset." That is just what I did.

I started calling attorneys, looking for one who would take my case. I found a city attorney who was an ex-prosecutor in the county DA's office. He actually knew my chief. When I told him my story, he was furious. He took my case pro-bono.

My attorney made mincemeat out of my chief and the department. They had to agree to return me to work. When my attorney told me we had won, he also issued a warning. "They're never going to let you live this down," he said. "You need to get another job."

I looked at him and said, "No way. This is my job."

The day I returned to work, I walked in with my head high even though I realized that everybody in that gossip-filled building knew too many details of my tortured youth, that they'd drawn unflattering conclusions based on their own self-righteousness. I used to admire these people; now I pitied them for their limited scope of compassion and ignorance.

Over the next years, I stayed there no matter how they tried to make my experience miserable. The chief and my superiors kept a fire to my ass. They clocked when I came in and when I left. They kept tabs on who I talked to and what I did, no matter how trivial. They constantly searched for ways to trip me up. They never found any.

I got little support from my peers and colleagues. It was a liability to stand too close to me. If someone stood in my office doorway to ask me a question, a supervisor was sure to ask them what they were doing there. "Is that who you hang with?" they'd ask. It was guilt by association. In law enforcement, there is little middle ground. You're on one side or the other. I didn't blame my peers for ditching me; they had their careers to think of, too.

I survived by thinking of my own career, constantly. I performed better than I had before. I still loved my job working with the clients the court personnel. I made them the focus of my time and energy—not the politics of the department. But I played the politics game when I had to. I made them promote me. For every promotion I received after the big to-do, they passed me over three times, until they couldn't ignore me anymore. The chief spent the reminder of his career in the department with his hand over my head keeping me from moving up. I had made him look bad, and he never forgave me. Near the end of my career, and right before he retired, he actually had me train the next supervisor—after he passed me over for that job.

I gutted it out not only because I loved my work, but because of my kids. They were going to school. They had a home and a community. I would have done anything to keep them from being uprooted. I set my sights on getting my twenty years in. After twenty years, you can retire and keep your medical and dental benefits for life. Those professional benefits are worth a lot.

I was able to stay, to thrive in my work in spite of the hostility directed at me, because of forgiveness. My chief, who tried to block me at every turn, who looked at me with disgust whenever he forced himself to look at me, was one of the easiest to forgive, ironically. It all comes down to understanding. I used to recite "Father forgive them for they know not what they do" nearly every day. He clearly didn't understand why he was so affronted by my presence—he probably wouldn't let himself think about it. Yes, I had damaged his ego—the rising star, who he had mentored and promoted, had disgraced him. He thought I had made him look foolish. But really what he could not forgive was that he had been mesmerized by me. He was this big macho Italian guy, and I was a little blonde girl who he thought he could protect and control. When he found out I had been a hooker, it offended his sense of himself. How could I be a hooker one decade and worthy of his respect several years later? He thought he was judging me, but he was really judging himself.

That was true of Clark too. When the problems with the department began and he learned the truth about my past, it was a shock, but he seemed to deal with it. Our marriage remained strong; our sex life was still good. But later, when he became a cop, my past became a much bigger deal. After all, nearly everyone knew about my past now—people don't forget a scandal like that. The judgment of his law enforcement colleagues infected Clark, and although he never reproached me, he had to deal with their judgments of him. Those judgments helped kill our marriage.

Here's the big lesson I learned from being a pariah—when someone judges you, it is never about you. It's always about them. When you know this, it is easier to forgive them and move on.

Reflections

Under the guise of righteousness, people do the strangest things, especially when they perceive their ego has been assaulted. Before I react to the righteous judgment of others—or before I righteously judge others myself—I find it helpful to stop and ask myself what I am reacting to. Where are my motives originating from? If they are coming from fear, selfishness, or the desire for revenge—I stop.

When someone offends or humiliates you, it's natural to lash out, to react by protecting yourself. You feel wronged. However, it's wise to stop and reflect before acting because, often, we concoct stories to make the person who hurt us into a villain. We design stories that will justify taking action against the offender. But these stories might not be true, and if you react to a false perception, you've limited your own power.

What if we forgave when we believed we were wronged? What if we practiced Jesus' principle of forgiving people their ignorance, and released the event—and the significance we attach to it—from our minds? We would no longer be shackled to our righteousness, our need to seek vindication would slip away. Our anger and fear would lose their power, and we would gain our own.

Through forgiveness, we give ourselves the freedom to continue living, loving and embracing the opportunities that, after all, are still out there, waiting for us to discover them.

QUESTIONS:

1) Define what forgiveness means to you, as both the giver and receiver.

2) Have you ever been misjudged despite your best intentions? Journal about a specific situation when your actions were misunderstood.

3) Recall a situation where you misjudged another and formed your opinion of a situation before having all the facts.

4) How easy or how difficult is it for you to forgive yourself for mistakes made? Give yourself an "I completely forgive you for everything" day at least once a week, and refuse to chastise yourself. How does it feel to love yourself unconditionally on that day?

CHAPTER THIRTEEN

STUBBORNLY MAKING A DIFFERENCE—OR NOT

*Once you are comfortable with your own pain,
you can become comfortable with the pain of others.*

Despite the antagonism directed against me in the Probation Department, I continued to rise. They could not deny that my performance was excellent, nor could they deny my dedication.

The truth is, I loved walking into court, jail cells and holding rooms every day, interviewing new clients, serving the justice system, and I continued to love it until I left law enforcement. The satisfaction didn't come from having great deal of power—although perhaps we did—but instead from knowing my contribution might create a last chance for one of my "cases" or closure for a victim. I had the opportunity to tell them the truth, straight. It may sound crazy – I got as much from it as I gave. I truly cared about the results of the case and the condition of the inmates and the victims lives. In the intricate bureaucratic world of the criminal justice system, I was a rarity. I had been on both sides, and I knew. I understood the value of being tough and compassionate, and how to regard human decency by separating the behavior (sometimes my own) from the person.

For the last 16 years on the job, I worked as a sentencing officer. I interviewed people once they'd been convicted or pleaded guilty to a crime, researched their cases, their lives, and prepared a detailed sentencing recommendation for the court. My recommendations could range from probation to twenty years, or more, of prison time. These recommendations carried a lot of weight with District Attorneys and judges, especially if you had a reputation for unvarnished honesty, which I did. The Public Defender attorneys were not as fond of me for the same reason. I wasn't there to make things easier on the clients; I was there to tally up and show them the factual consequences of their behavior.

I handled this the way I handled the kids in Juvenile Hall tough but compassionate. I did not allow any room at all for excuses, but I always considered it important to know, and for my clients to know, how they got themselves into crime. Not to justify their behavior, but to understand it. Without understanding, they were unlikely to accept responsibility for their actions. To let them make excuses, to minimize or dismiss their involvement in their own lives narrowed their vision into the future. If we don't connect our actions to the consequences, it's a lot less likely we'll correct the behavior that got us there.

People are funny. We shrink from hearing the truth about ourselves, but, ultimately, we like it. No one likes being lied to. My ability to tell people the truth without judgment was the hallmark of my success in my field.

I've never believed that someone's crimes define who they are. When you label people, the label obscures the person, you don't see the human being anymore. You just see the label.

Being non-judgmental was key. I never believed I was any better than my clients, no matter what they'd done. Yes, we are responsible for our behavior, but our behavior is not who we are at the core. We are all human beings trying to get along the best we can. Some of us just figured out how to do it sooner or with greater ease than others.

I often interviewed people who had schizoid tendencies or various mental disorders, who came in literally wearing tin foil on their heads. I would say to them, "Who are you waiting to hear from? What are they saying?" I wasn't talking down to them; I really wanted to know. I wanted them to tell me their stories so I could understand what was going on in their chemistry and understand the delusions that were so important to them. When I was in my teens, I took acid like everyone else in San Francisco; I think that what they were experiencing must have been sort of like an acid trip. They were operating on multiple distorted levels. I knew a fraction of what that was like.

I didn't work with many prostitution cases, since I usually worked with male offenders, but the women I did deal with who had prostitution in their records were not primarily prostitutes. They were drug addicts. When I was on the street, Gene did not allow me to use drugs; he demanded I keep my body in impeccable condition. By the time I entered law enforcement, street life had changed. The girls on the street were barely conscious. Actually, doing drugs is not that much different than selling your body. You're dishonoring yourself either way. How could I judge them? I'd been there, too.

Even later in my career, when I worked at San Quentin interviewing felons and those designated "high risk" offenders, I didn't label them. Whenever I walked into a holding cell, I was always conscious that had it not been for the grace of God, it could have been me waiting there.

My reputation as tough and tell-it-straight preceded me into the cells. I can't tell you how many times I walked into a jail and overheard this exchange:

Bailiff: "Your sentencing officer is here to see you."

Prisoner: "Which one is it?"

Bailiff: "Bonelli."

Prisoner: "Oh, shit."

It wasn't always that way. Before I earned my reputation, or with guys who didn't know me, many of the men would take one look at me—blond, female—and they'd start these show-off flirtation games, or call me "Ma'am" with a smirk. I'd glare at them and slam their file down on the table, and say, "Let's back up the truck, bud. First of all, this isn't about me. It's not about how I see you. It's not about anything you have to say about me, my history or reputation." I'd look at the police report and say, "This is about April 3rd at 3:30 p.m. when you robbed that store at gunpoint. That's what we're here to talk about. If you want to talk about it, let's carry on. If you don't, I'm out of here."

I knew where the inmates were coming from. They were in survival mode, and I remembered it well. I knew what they wanted: They wanted to get out. They would lie and tell me they lived somewhere they didn't; they would flirt, bat their eyes and expect me to buy anything. It was nothing but bullshit, manipulation, Red Zone residents perfecting their con. It worked on some of the officers. If an officer had an ego that was not intact, the guys would work their manipulation expertly. It seldom worked on me.

When I talked to guys I knew were users (which was most of them), I'd just be blunt and ask "What's your drug of choice?" I didn't ask open-ended questions like, "How long have you been using?" That was just asking to be lied to. I already knew they used, so I saved them face. They didn't have to feel shamed by revealing something that was hard for them to face. It was already revealed.

When I entered the interview room with a high-risk offender (3-striker), the guards shackled both their arms and legs. My god, what a production, just to bring a guy into an interview room. The guards were big men, and two of them would escort the inmate to see me, treating him like he was the big bad wolf. A guard would unshackle his legs, then ask me if I needed the inmate's hands free for anything before he'd unshackle his arms. The guards were trying to impress me, too. I found all the theatrical posturing silly.

Once the guard left, the prisoner would look me over, then huff, puff, grunt and grimace. I'd say, "Are you done?" He would maybe cock his eyebrow at me. I'd say, "Did you stare in the mirror for a long time to perfect that look? What's up?"

"If you want to get involved in your life, you can," I'd tell him. "You decide. What do you want to do? How do you want to play this? It's your call. It's your life. It's your file. It's your freedom. We're here to talk about you, what are you gonna tell me?"

I made them talk about themselves, about the stuff they'd done. I never let them do their con. I encouraged them to own their lives, to understand they'd made choices, and the choices led them to that room and the shackles. Perhaps this was the first and only time they'd ever been able to do that. Instead of letting them go on about "poor me, or if hadn't been for.." I had them thinking about "now what?"

Someone once asked whether I saw a common denominator among people caught in the criminal justice system. I did. It wasn't socio-economics or race; it was that they didn't graduate from high school. That was the one thing I could almost guarantee I'd see when I took a guy's history. He gave up on his future a long time ago.

It seems funny to say about men who were going to prison, some of them for a long time, but I encouraged hope for a future. I let them know that their future was up to them, right here and right now. Prison was where they were in that moment, but it was up to them what they learned from it. They could choose how their future played out.

I remember one guy, a true sociopath who had abused so many for so many years. His final offense, which earned him a sentence of 25 years, was egregious animal cruelty. "You've gotten away with so many excuses," I told him. "But it's not your parents, girlfriend, school, teacher, mother, or stepfather. The only thing that impacts you is what you get out of any given situation. The rest of your life is going to be in an institution because it's the only place where you can find direct behavior modification. You screw up, and you go to the holding cell. You deviate and something will get taken away from you. Out in society there are too many things you can manipulate." He just stared at me while I talked. He knew somewhere inside, it was the truth.

"Let's think about how you're going to spend your time from now on," I said. "How can you find some source within yourself that will help you grow?" When he was silent, I said, "When you want to be real and talk about what you're going to do with the next twenty years of your life, you tell the guard to call me, and I'll come back down. I'm not here to play games with you." And he said, "No. You don't have to leave."

Most guys responded to my tough stance. They felt relieved, I think, to not to have to play their games, to tell the truth of their story, and to have someone affirm they did not have to be defined by the story. There was always some pivotal experience from their developmental years they'd never resolved. I'd say, "This isn't about you now. This is about you then. Let's go back and talk about you then." They'd say, "What are you, a counselor or psychiatrist?" And I'd say, "I'm just somebody who cares so you don't keep having to do the same shit over and over, man. Aren't you tired?" They'd say, "Yes."

Most of them were crying by the time I left the holding cell. They'd thank me profusely. It didn't matter how "bad" their crime was. I'd let them know their crime was not the sum of who they were.

Sometimes I'd talk to the guys who had molested children. "You must really hate yourself," I'd say. "It has to feel like shit. You're damned if you do, and damned if you don't. You have this affinity for little boys, and nobody likes you for it. You don't like yourself for it. And you can't change it. So what can you do with this energy?"

Allowing people to be who they are is a huge gift. Remove the pretenses, and they can start again, on a firmer foundation this time. At least that's my hope.

Starting again didn't mean they could forget what they did. They had to start again where they were—usually prison. They'd always ask me what I was going to recommend. I'd never sugar coat it. If it was going to be a long stint, I'd tell them the truth. I would say, "I'd like to tell you it'll be different, but it isn't going to happen. You have to go down. Now what you can do, from this conversation on, is build your life from wherever you are. You need to find out what you believe in. I don't care if it's Allah or Jesus, but you need to start getting straight with who you are and how you're living, because this is the rest of your life."

People talk a lot about treating others with respect. But I didn't treat the inmates with respect—respect must be earned, and their behavior showed they hadn't earned mine. I did treat them with dignity, which is different than respect. When you honor someone's dignity, it means they are a real person to you, not some piece of trash you can throw away. I cared for my clients' lives when I asked them, "What are you going to learn from this experience? I'm here with you right now and right now I give a shit. There's nothing else going on in my life but me being here with you right now. I want to know about your life and how you got here. I want to help you figure out what you can do to stay out of here. If you want to take the time to be concerned about yourself with me at your side, I'm here now." Then it was up to them.

I was a straight shooter in the other part of my job, too—when I dealt with the judges and the attorneys. So many of the people I interviewed were people who knew how to manipulate the system. They built their lives on excuses. I felt we should strip away the excuses and just let them be with themselves to make it or break it. We didn't need to add any more bullshit of our own. That was the attitude I carried with me when I entered a courtroom.

Most of the judges appreciated me, and all of them respected me. I never danced around all the egos present in the courtroom; I talked straight. I didn't play the "this guy is a poor victim" card, or the "this guy shows no remorse" card. I just talked about where they were, where they were headed, and what they had done. When I walked into a courtroom, the judge was often happy to see me.

Judges are human, too, with their own perceptions and opinions. I learned all their quirks. One judge worked with Mothers Against Drunk Driving, and she threw the book at drunk driving cases. Another judge tended to be lenient with sex offenders, I don't know why. Maybe he liked porn himself. One judge had zero tolerance for embezzlers, although another judge would go light on them. But I never met a judge who didn't care about what he or she was doing. They honored their power over other peoples' lives. I never met one who abused that power.

The defense attorneys had a different focus. They had such huge case loads, all they really wanted was to dispose of a case as soon as they could. The District Attorneys liked me in court because I was no-nonsense and my goal was the same as theirs: put this guy where he needs to be.

As a law enforcement officer, I upheld the laws. That doesn't mean I don't think some of them are bullshit. I was a probation officer when California passed the Three Strikes law, and I became the premier sentence officer of three-strike litigation throughout the state. And I think that law was totally wrong. I spent a lot of time trying to mitigate its effects.

Under the Three Strikes law, once someone was convicted of three so-called "serious" felonies, they had to be sentenced to at least 25 years in prison. It was disproportional. It prevented the courts and law enforcement from using their professional judgment. If a person fit the narrow criteria of the law, they went to prison for 25 years at least, period. But politicians crafted the criteria, and they did so without consulting any front line law enforcement professionals.

That law set up law enforcement. For wardens and corrections officers, it took away work-time and good behavior credit, removing a tool they'd used to get criminals to comply with daily routines. The criminals weren't stupid; they knew that three strikes meant that no matter how they behaved in prison, they were there for 25 years. And the law tied the hands of the cops on the street, too. If a cop pulled over a motorist, and that motorist knew he already had two qualifying priors, meaning he's now a three-striker, he's not likely to go gracefully. He just might put up a fight. But the cop won't know that up front, so he's likely to get hurt.

The only people who thought the Three Strikes law worked were the voters who duped themselves into believing they were getting rid of the dregs of society. They were wrong. That law just created more room for violence.

The worst thing about the Three Strikes law is that it killed any possibility of redemption for the criminals. I fought against the law in one particular case with all my strength, and lost. My client was a guy who was raised by a crack addict mother, and who spent his entire, short life in trouble. He was not a great guy. When he was eighteen, he stole a bicycle out of someone's garage, and was convicted of residential burglary. After that, he started boosting, meaning he stole clothes from places like Mervyns or Sears. Boosters wear girdles and straps under their clothes, carry hangers between their legs, carry bags and backpacks, all for the purpose of theft. When he was caught, he had over $700 worth of merchandise, which raised his crime up from petty theft to grand theft. On the way out of the store, he pocketed someone's wallet. The two crimes of Burglary and Robbery qualified him for a 25-year prison sentence under the Three Strikes law, if he was ever convicted again of another felony.

His third strike was for perjury. He refused to testify in a Drug case, maintaining that if he testified against the accused drug dealer, he would be murdered. Everyone in law enforcement knew he wasn't making a phony excuse, but telling the truth. The D.A. didn't care and, when my client refused to testify, charged and convicted him of perjury. Since that was his third strike, my client was sent to prison for 25 years. He was 22 years old.

This guy had no chance. I was so fucking upset. I argued against the D.A. in court, summoning the ferocity I once used to defend myself. Still, I lost. The law favored the D.A. So we sent a 22-year-old kid to jail for 25 years for stealing a bike, a bunch of clothes, and refusing to let himself be murdered. This was justice? It didn't matter if, we believed he wasn't a threat to anyone's safety. It didn't matter whether, in the judge's opinion, he would be better off in a treatment program. None of it mattered. What mattered was we took away whatever was remaining of his life. We took away his chance at recovery and redemption. We didn't see him as a person. Under the Three Strikes law, he was just a case.

Thank God the Three Strikes law has been changed now, and is not so rigid. Now the state allows the courts to strike the priors, or to reduce the crimes to misdemeanors in mitigating circumstances. I'm glad I raised my voice about this law, even if it did make me temporarily unpopular with the D.A.s.

I came full circle with my career when I became a Training Officer, traveling the state to teach other officers interviewing techniques, determining sentencing, enhancing self-esteem, and working with the Three Strikes law. A couple of times I found myself teaching officers who had been juvenile counselors when I'd been a juvenile within the system. When they realized who I was, it gave them a jolt. Many veteran officers don't see the possibility of redemption. They no longer care about the people they serve; they've burnt out. They mostly just care about getting through to retirement. I hope that when they saw me, one of their forgotten cases, they woke up to the possibility of redemption. Maybe. Or maybe not.

People have asked me if I feel good about the people I "helped." I didn't help anybody. They helped themselves. All I gave them was the opportunity to believe in themselves. This was part of my own soul work.

They didn't always take that opportunity. I'd be with a guy in the holding cell, he's crying, I'm listening. He'd thank me a hundred times. He had a plan on how to get his life straight. I'd recommend probation, and forty-five days later, where is he? Back doing the same shit. But that had nothing to do with me.

That's where people get mixed up. They'd say, "A lot of good you did." I'd say, "I did what I was supposed to do. He may come back fifty times. He may die trying, but that doesn't mean I don't show up being all I can be." What I can be, not him. He's the only one responsible for him. I'm the only one responsible for me.

In 2009, I received a six-page, hand-written letter from a guy I only vaguely remember. He was on my case load in 2001 and 2002. I often had 200 people on my case load at any one time, so it's not surprising I don't remember him. "I would like you to hear a story of the positive impact of your actions," the letter began. "I am sure you know your reputation among the defense bar. When I came to you, my attorney said to be completely open, that you were likely to write a report so harsh that it could be discounted. You probed my history, including three or four prior prison terms, but also my two BA degrees, and my alcohol abuse. We spent several hours together in that first meeting, and I had been through the system enough to know this is unusual. You told me firmly but gently that I absolutely had to stop drinking if I wanted a better, a different, life. You gave me a card, said you couldn't make me go to AA, but said I must for myself. I was shocked at your compassion and that you used my openness to try to help rather than to try to hurt me. It was especially shocking considering your reputation. Your reaction to my openness, to my admissions of dishonesty, fear, weaknesses, was life-changing—even if not immediately so."

The letter goes on to tell of his continued problems with stealing, drinking on and off, and more prison time. But at the time he wrote to me, he'd been sober for more than a year and his propensity to steal had been restrained. His biggest threat these days is complacency. That is why he wrote the letter. In his last paragraph, he says: "You are the person that changed the direction of my life. It was a curve, not an abrupt U-turn. That is sad for me, but the fact is that the ultimate result was life changing for me. If I had been assigned to a different PO in 2001, I might very well be different today. At the time, you surely thought your efforts had failed. I want you to know that at least one seeming failure actually became a stunning success. I am grateful beyond words, and I want you to know it."

Of course, it feels good to get a letter like that. I've been around long enough to know that he might go back to drinking and stealing—so many do. That's up to him. But at least he had a year of hope, and that right there gives him an opening to do a whole lot more.

We advocate random acts of kindness. Often unknown to us are the effects of the outcome. Changing our condition begins with changing ourselves then extending a hand to others through random acts of service.

Reflections

We are the sum of those experiences we have lived, but we need not be defined by them. I often think of each experience as an isolated event. The challenge is to see it as something external instead of internalizing it and allowing it to determine who we are.

When we make a mistake, or suffer a loss, it can expose pieces of ourselves, some attractive, some unattractive. Being able to see ourselves clearly enables us to choose our responses to these events.

Fear will often be our first response, and sometimes it's necessary. But if fear is the only response, it cultivates dysfunction. We can choose to move past fear, to embrace love. Love lets us move past our sorrows, it widens our hearts, nurtures our soul, and encourages our endurance.

We are responsible for what we choose. And, as time moves on, we get chances to choose again. When you choose fear, it's easy to lock onto it and disconnect. Or, you can choose a different response.

In 1994, California voters chose fear and passed the Three Strikes law. More than a decade later, they revised that decision. The client who wrote to me chose to keep drinking. Seven years later, he made a different choice.

It starts with acknowledging we have a choice. Once we do that, we can choose love, or forgiveness, or understanding. Or all three. The key is to learn to love ourselves.

> *When the event we're reacting to is one of suffering, pain or loss, we become bigger when we accept those feelings, rather than suppressing them. Excuses and blame keep us small. It is easy to say love is letting go, but how do we do that in the throes of suffering, or when our survival is on the line? Perhaps if we trust that the Divine created the experience to transform us, we could offer thanks in the face of loss, neglect, or even sadness.*
>
> *My life, my decisions, gave me a deep well of experiences to draw on, and each one showed me various pieces of myself. As I confronted each one, I had to view them with compassion and love—for me. The harder it was for me to do that, the greater my triumph when I succeeded, and the greater the lesson. Once we allow ourselves to experience the event, then choose a behavior from love, true growth begins.*

QUESTIONS:

1) Where in your life are you stubbornly making a difference?

_____

_____

_____

2) Are you defining yourself by a particular experience in your life? Is it time to have a broader definition of who you are? How would you like to be known today?

_____

_____

_____

3) Today be conscious of the motivation behind your decisions. Work to make choices that cultivate more love in your life for yourself and for people you care about. Perhaps you will want to keep a 24-hour journal of how this plays out and the positive outcomes.

CHAPTER FOURTEEN

EVERYONE WANTS A PIECE OF ME

*Broken dreams are new opportunities to create triumph
by setting new intentions.*

A fog descended around me during my divorce from Clark. I invested so much in our relationship that when he left, I left too. I left myself.

Those old feelings of being disposable returned, as did the pain, and despite all I'd learned, I locked myself away with my hurt and self pity. I even shut out my kids, who were reeling from Clark's rejection of them. I struggled to show up, even for my youngest daughter Gina, who was only ten years old and needed me. Their pain only magnified mine. The one place I allowed myself to really show up was my job, where I could concentrate on other people's pain instead of my own.

This episode lasted nearly two years, two years of worrying how I was going to live my life alone, consumed by the idea that, at 42, I would never find a man to stand with me. I didn't see how I could find one who would measure up to Clark anyway, at least the Clark from the golden years of our marriage. That time was over, and the realization of this fact swamped me with grief.

In short, I was a mess. But eventually I emerged, and from all the soul searching and anguish I had gone through, I thought I emerged stronger. I believed I could be my own greatest resource, and that I didn't need Clark or anyone else to validate my existence. I believed in a power greater than myself, and I had learned to depend on that power for support.

Or so I thought.

In reality, my gut told a less rosy story. When I was alone, the old doubts assailed me—I wouldn't survive on my own. These doubts manifested themselves in my old adversary, the panic attack.

After all I'd endured, and the growth I'd worked so hard to accomplish, I believed I was enlightened, so faith-filled. Yet there I was, doubled over in the grocery store, gasping for breath. It was the toughest lesson of all for me: to believe I was loveable without someone else validating me.

And just like my other big life lessons, the teacher I chose was not a mentor or a wise man. He wasn't even a nice guy.

About two years after the split with Clark, I started getting out again, having fun with girlfriends, developing some kind of social life. I wasn't looking for a relationship; I thought I'd given up hope for that.

One evening my girlfriend and I were having dinner at a restaurant we frequented. We were sitting at the bar waiting for a table, laughing with the bartender and other patrons—I knew everybody there, and they all knew me. A new guy walked in, and our eyes met. I know how corny this sounds, but electricity passed between us. He was a tall, handsome guy; he looked a lot like Tom Selleck. He sat down at a table across from us and took a file folder out of his briefcase—it looked like he was going to meet a client or something. But every few seconds he'd glance at me, and I looked at him, passing non-verbal messages to each other. Even when his client came, and my girlfriend and I moved to a table for dinner, we continued to flirt back and forth. It was exciting, and soothing to my suffering ego.

We had our after-dinner drinks in front of us, when my girlfriend went to the restroom. At the same time, his client got up and left. He came over and laid his hand on top of mine, as it rested by my glass. "Is it okay if I do this?" he asked, but it wasn't a question. He knew it was okay. His high degree of confidence startled me. Most guys are nervous around me.

In a nutshell, I was dazzled—by his looks, his confident manner, and his total focus on me. We were the last to leave the restaurant, and then we sat in the parking lot talking for another couple of hours. He seemed elated to find me.

Yes, I am aware how very similar that sentence about this man, Kurt, is to what I've written about meeting Gene. It's no accident.

I was wounded and lost again, much as I had been when I was seventeen, in spite of my successful profession, four wonderful kids, and a support system of friends. That's what attracted Kurt to me: my wounds. He had a built-in radar system for finding them. It was his single greatest talent.

For the next couple of months, he took me on a rocket ride. Soon he had moved in with me. "I want to give you the life you deserve," he said. "I want to be there for you for everything." I told him about how Clark had treated me in the last years of our marriage, and he got really angry on my behalf. Kurt could huff and puff like a linebacker. I felt like I had been sick for a long time and Kurt gave me the right medicine. I lapped up his strength and adoration like a hungry dog.

He pushed to get married. I resisted at first, because I was uneasy with the speed we were travelling. But I was moved by his passion for me, his ability to sense my wants without me having to ask, his doting interest in everything and everyone around me. He wanted me so badly!

So I agreed to get married. I told myself I loved him.

I wasn't totally bamboozled, though. I noticed he didn't drink alcohol and asked him about it; he confessed he was an alcoholic but claimed he'd been sober for five years. He seemed so honest and remorseful as he told me about his ex-wife and how they'd split up because of his drinking. They had two little kids together, so the next time we were arranging a kid swap, I thought I'd try to get an idea just how bad his drinking had been. I asked Barbara, his ex-wife, why they got divorced.

"I got tired of not having sex," Barbara said. My mouth fell open in shock. Kurt pawed me all day long. I used to tell him I had to get more sleep if I was going to make it to work on time. It was so hard to reconcile her description with the Kurt I knew.

Maybe she wasn't attractive to him, I thought. But when I told Kurt what Barbara had said, he just shrugged and said pregnancy and childbirth turned him off. Well, that was weird, too. When I was pregnant with Gina, her birth brought Clark and me closer together. But who was I to judge? Everyone has their own prejudices. Everyone gets to be who they are. And since I wasn't going to have any more children, Kurt's strange reaction would have no bearing on our sex life. Right?

We got married. And everything changed. Kurt relaxed into the man he really was. Now that the deal had been sealed and he was safe, he took off his mask.

It would be tiresome here to relate Kurt's story as it pertains to mine. The opportunistic man who preyed on the needs of a vulnerable woman—it's such an old story it's a cliché. Besides, telling his story gives him more importance than he's worth. Let's cut it short. Once we married, I found out Kurt was a shopaholic: he spent money like water, although he wasn't generous—everything he bought was for himself. He was jealous of my co-workers and my girlfriends, and accused me of favoring them over him. From overly doting, he became critical of me and everything about me. I was too independent, too bossy, too demanding, too sexy.

He started wearing strong after-shave, and long before I was sure of it, I suspected he had begun drinking again. Those five years of sobriety? Fiction.

Of course, he suddenly lost interest in sex. We probably had sex all of five times in the first two years of our marriage. His ex-wife's words echoed in my head. It wasn't her. It wasn't me. It was him.

He was a man with a huge hole in himself. After I finally stopped pretending to myself that I loved him, I felt sorry for him. I didn't want to be a failure at marriage so I tried to fill his holes by remaking myself into the woman he thought he wanted, but of course I failed.

After I retired from law enforcement, I took my savings, my pension, and the money my father had left me (he died about six months after Kurt and I got married), and because I thought a drastic change might be good for Kurt and help to save our marriage, I bought property in Maui. We moved. It didn't help. In fact, it got worse.

He drained my money, drained my energy, and drained my soul. We lived in a toxic atmosphere of lies. He made promises about everything, and broke every one of them, lied about it, and blamed all our troubles on me. Our money—my money—disappeared in strange ways. We moved back to California for another "fresh start," although I kept the property in Maui and rented it out. Nothing changed.

I persevered for five long years because I couldn't bear to admit that I had made a very bad mistake, and had failed—again—at love. Finally, I told Kurt we had to get a divorce. I wanted to keep it simple and as friendly as possible, but he panicked. He tried to drain my property (and nearly succeeded); he opened a line of credit based on my assets and went on a huge spending spree, including buying a new car; he tried to blackmail me with doctored recordings of me that he'd been making for years (!); he tried to sue me for most everything I owned. Since all his claims were false, none of them stuck for long. They cost me mammoth amounts of money and legal fees and this bought him time.

He gained financial leverage, which he used to hook another victim. And this is where this sorry story has a happy ending. When I finally became aware of the depths of his betrayals and manipulation, my main emotions were shame and guilt. How could I have been so foolish for so long, and allowed myself to be used in this way? I was an experienced, savvy, law enforcement professional. I prided myself on being able to see a man's game before he even opened his mouth. Yet a glib con man took me for a ride. The sentence that haunted me was: I should have known.

I wallowed in my guilt and shame for a several weeks. I came dangerously close to seeing myself as a victim, which I'd never done before, not even when I was on the street. I shuffled around my house, crying "How could someone do this?" Until my daughter Tara spoke up. "Get your game face on, Mom," she said. "You've got to fight fire with fire."

For some reason this got through to me—maybe because it was my daughter who said it. This was not just about me. I was still my children's mother, and how I behaved in times of adversity would always serve as a model for them. I needed to show them what you do when you get knocked down. You get up.

To prepare for divorce court and all of Kurt's trumped-up lies, I embarked on a journey into his past. Guess what I found? I wasn't the only one. He didn't have just one estranged ex-wife; he had five. I was the sixth wife to suffer huge losses. All of us shared a similar story of financial loss and physical rejection shortly after the "wedding." Some still struggled to understand what they did wrong.

I tracked all five of them down. I unearthed all the records from each place they'd been married, figured out their maiden names, traced their current addresses, got their phone numbers, and began calling them. One had died. The other four were all professional women: one had been a mortgage consultant, and one was even a staff member in the District Attorney's office. All had been swept off their feet by Kurt's intense focus on their desires, and his unerring ability to zero in on their wounds. All found out after marriage that he wasn't what he had seemed. Except for Barbara, who was the only one who'd had kids by him, and myself, none of them had been married more than two years. All of them had been used and betrayed and ripped off; all of them were bitter and angry.

None of them knew each other until I gathered us all together. The first time we got together for dinner, man did we bond. It was like an instant sisterhood. It was so empowering to know that other women—successful, intelligent, accomplished women—had been lured down the same path. It wasn't us—it was him. Why should we feel ashamed because we had wounds? Who doesn't have wounds? In each other's company, we could see Kurt was the one who was truly disabled.

Maybe the best part of meeting the ex-wives was in preventing another woman from becoming Number Seven. Through my contacts in law enforcement, and his ex-wife in the District Attorney's office, we discovered Kurt was reeling in someone else, planning to marry again as soon as his divorce from me was final. She was another professional woman. The DA's assistant and another former wife called her and told her who and what Kurt was. Of course she didn't believe it—she was enamored with Kurt, just as all of us had been at first. She was preparing to move in with him—into my house, which he deceived her into thinking was his. Kurt was so thoughtful, she said, he was the perfect guy she'd been looking for all her life. We listened, we empathized, and we told her we had proof.

Our professions gave us enough authority to convince her to meet with us, and when she did, we showed her everything.

Disillusion broke her heart, and it was painful to watch. But how much worse it would have been two years later, after he'd burrowed his way into her life and leached all he could from her bank accounts and her soul. Instead, we took her from him. It felt good.

Of course, there will be another Number Seven. Or maybe he's on Number Eight by now. As long as there are wounded women, and Kurt can breathe, there will be more. After my court battle with Kurt, I got my house back. Two of my "ex-wife sisters," who accompanied me to court, came with me to re-enter my house and see what Kurt had left behind. We found a stack of photos from women he'd met online. He'd made detailed notes on the back of each photo—when he'd met them, what his impressions were of them, what they were looking for, and when he was planning to call them back. Along with his personal rating. It was chilling to see the advance preparation he had made. Oh yes, I'm sure he's not done.

Predators lurk everywhere, and they're not all like Gene, jumping out from behind garbage cans to attack you. You have to be careful who you marry. Yet, do I want to become suspicious, viewing every man with narrowed eyes? I don't think so. I know I have a little girl naiveté that tries to see the good in people. Even though it hasn't always served me well, I'm not willing to let it go. I believe it is a gift. I just have to hone my skills.

When I think of marriage, I now believe I only had one, with Clark. Clark and I had good times and bad times, but it was always a marriage. I don't think of the relationship with Kurt as a marriage. If anything, it was dating with a license. Still, this, too, gave me an opportunity to grow. I saw how easy it was for me to lose myself in a relationship, how easy it was for me to discard my instincts in the hope of being loved—something we all want. And I hope I now know how to preserve my gift for finding the good in people without squelching my intuition and abandoning myself.

Reflections

Even when we do the wrong things for the wrong reasons, if we are courageous enough to search the wreckage for the pieces that led to our own self-deception, we can salvage something valuable.

In my relationship with Kurt, no matter what I gave it was never enough, and it never would be. Although I worked constantly on my own issues of self-worth, the negativity surrounding me eroded whatever gains I made. I felt as though I was filling my bathtub with warm fragrant water, but before I could get in to enjoy it, someone else pulled the plug. Over time, I realized I'd surrendered my self-esteem to someone completely incapable of nurturing me or even himself. His self doubt was so strong it magnified my own. I questioned my ability in all areas of my life. Humans are porous; we are influenced by whatever is present and consistent in our world. We have to pick wisely what—or who—will share our space.

When I have lost at love, it churns up the wreckage from my past. My issues with abandonment, fear of not being good enough, rejection, and a sense of being lost, surface in my soul. Only in relationships have I found a sense of safety and value.

Many of us grew up believing that if we modified our appearance or behavior toward others, people would treat us better, our lives would change. In truth, the only thing that needs to change is our commitment to ourselves. We learned to "put a lid on it," to avoid conflict with others. In truth, we need to see conflict as an opportunity to better our lives, and to stand firm when it comes our way. We learned to worry about someone else's reaction rather than represent our own needs. In truth, we were telling others, "I'm not that important," and the issues that trouble us, that deserve a conversation, continue to recur, like hiccups out of nowhere that we cannot control.

Once we stop avoiding conflict, we can begin to get comfortable with how to approach it, using the tools of truth and self-love. By confronting the truth about my relationship with Kurt, I discovered a network of women who supported me in a time of crisis and pain. Together, we helped prevent Kurt from hurting another woman. My confidence grew back, and so did my self-respect.

To deny ourselves is like swimming in the sea and letting the riptide pull you out. Life is full of choppy waves, murky waters, and sharks. That is a fact. Our challenge is develop a stroke that suits our personal style so that we may swim freely and without fear.

QUESTIONS:

1) How often do you think people are totally truthful about themselves and their motives in relationship?"

_____

_____

_____

_____

_____

_____

_____

2. Is there any aspect of your current relationship that you need to get real with yourself about?

CHAPTER FIFTEEN

LET'S MAKE A DEAL

Nothing replaces the human touch.

Perhaps the reason I did not scorn Kurt's need to shop and buy, shop and buy, was because I suffered from a variant of this same addictive behavior. Mine took the form of seeking out, and never passing up a "good deal."

It had nothing to do with whether I had money. If I had money, my good deals might have a higher total price tag, that's all. It wasn't even about the actual stuff. Many times I didn't need what I bought.

The buzz didn't come from the goods—it came from the "good buy." It upped the ante. I loved the hunt for bargains, the thrill of a negotiation, and the rush from closing a deal.

On my first trip to Europe, I visited Venice, Italy, a city famous for its canals, arched stone bridges and architecture; a city chocked full of fine opportunities for shopaholics to feed their addiction. One day I took a ferry from Venice to the quaint island of Murano, known for its ancient tradition of glass-blowing. I wanted something to commemorate my trip abroad, something unique and beautiful. A glass-blown vase would be perfect, I thought. In Murano, I found a high-end glass shop where every piece was a hand-blown one-of-a kind. So far, I'm just another ordinary tourist, right? A glow stole over me, one that did not come from being surrounded by beautiful works hand-crafted by master artisans. No, it came from my strategizing how to get one (or more) of those pieces for less than what the glass-blower wanted. They expected me to play the game, I told myself, and I was eager to participate.

My dance began. First, I selected a number of expensive items, all of them beautiful, any one of which would make a great souvenir. I asked for a "package price" on all the items, figuring the shop proprietor would be willing to bargain to avoid losing such a big sale. When he gave me his price for the list of items I'd picked out—which was about the cost of an economy car—I stepped back and said I'd have to think about it. I waited for a bit, then put some of the items back on the shelves. "How about now?" I asked.

He gave me a lesser (in relative terms) price, intimating that he was going below what he should. Another familiar feeling came over me—the compulsion to have those items, especially since now I knew it was a good deal. I duped myself into believing that I deserved to have them: my negotiating skills earned me a price deduction, so I'd proved I was worthy of them. The alternative would have been to say "No thanks" and leave the shop, but by then, I was well beyond rational thinking. "Deal," I said, taking the items at a thirty percent savings overall (the price of a fur coat). I came, I saw, I conquered, and I felt very grand, for a while.

In reality, of course, I'd conquered nothing at all. I spent thousands of dollars for the experience of combining self-indulgence, greed, and entitlement. What a great recipe for self-destruction.

This unwelcome piece of self-knowledge burbled up when I came home from Europe and put the glass-blown vases on my dining room table. No doubt—they were beautiful, refracting the light from the windows into a shimmering array of color. But their beauty brought me no pleasure, or even a glimmer of satisfaction from buying them for less than they were worth. Instead the light reflected by those vases seemed to show me the truth about my conduct, and in place of pleasure or satisfaction I felt a kind of disgust—with myself.

Addicts call this hitting bottom. You suddenly come face to face with an unattractive truth about yourself. You can either turn away, rationalize it or pretend you haven't seen it (which always leads to more self-destruction), or you wake up and start making some radical changes.

I tried rationalization, at first. I discussed my liking for good deals with friends, who agreed that getting a deal was a bonus in shopping. I glossed over the fact that I enjoyed the acquisition much more than the ownership. If an item was on sale, I wanted a greater discount. If I bought something online, I wanted free shipping. I refused to buy things that weren't on sale or when I couldn't negotiate a mark-down. I even sought out my deals in places like Macy's or Costco, so it wasn't like I limited my bargain hunting to luxury items.

And, hey, I told myself, I'd never brought myself to the brink of financial extinction. I wasn't an addict. I was thrifty.

These rationalizations all were partly true, but they didn't mean I didn't have an addiction. They just made it harder to diagnose. When I came home from Murano and placed those truly exorbitant vases on my table, they provided tangible proof that I had a problem. I could not hide from it any longer.

It is often said that ignorance is bliss. I disagree. I welcome knowledge and awareness, and once I realize something in me is out of balance, I am compelled to ask myself what I'm truly committed to. I didn't like the person who bought those vases, and I no longer wanted her to be part of me.

Addictions are always about filling a void with whatever substitute is available. Addictions are about emptiness. I knew this better than most people, because my work brought me into intimate contact with many addicts.

Getting a good deal said I was valuable. It filled up the empty space I'd had since my under-valued childhood. A good deal said, "You are worth something." This became an emotional fix for me. The more savvy I became at getting good deals, the more committed I became to the reward result. This is the mark of any addiction.

Like any other addiction, the cure wasn't magic. It was hard work, especially that first step—admitting I had a problem. And it didn't get easier as I undertook the mundane, daily work of changing my behavior. People think that understanding the "why" behind the behavior will immediately cure the behavior, but that's not true. In fact you really don't get the "why" until the behavior is gone. Change often must come first.

What could I do differently? The answer was to make myself buy things at cost. Ouch! I didn't change what I bought (except, of course, no more hand-blown vases); I changed how I bought. If something was marked $30.00, I paid $30.00. I ignored sales. I paid for shipping when buying online. I weaned myself from the reward buzz.

Was it hard? Yes. But in time the difficulties eased, and my focus shifted. Now I paid attention to what I actually purchased. Did I want the items? Need them? Were they worth my hard-earned dollars? My previous raw pleasure in shopping disappeared along with the buzz. Now when I look at the items I have selected, I do so in awareness and not in some self-deceptive haze. My satisfaction is in their usefulness, not in the conquest of a bargain.

I still have those vases. They are no longer souvenirs of my success in getting a good deal; they are a souvenir of my determination to change. They are far more beautiful now.

Reflections

Addiction is self-slavery. We use our reasoning ability to justify self-destructive conduct, to lie to ourselves about our motives.

For years, I walked into jail cells and confronted addicts, told them their lives would never improve until they admitted they had a problem. Then I hit the after-Christmas sale at Filene's Basement. My rationalizations not only concealed my problem, they prevented me from seeing I was in need.

I know now my quest for deals was really a search for recognition. I needed to be recognized as worthy, as having value—and not just by someone else, but in my own eyes.

I am worthy. I have enough. I deserve the best. Even when I don't believe these things, I act as if I do. I change my behavior first. It really does work.

QUESTIONS

1) Think of an addictive behavior you have and the feelings underneath it. What uncomfortable emotion do you try to suppress when you are caught in an addictive choice? How would it feel to sit with this emotion and not act? There is more about this process explained in Raphael Cushnir's wonderful book, The One Thing Holding You Back: Unleashing the Power of Emotional Connection.

_____

_____

_____

2) What addictive behaviors did you witness around you while you were growing up? What are you witnessing now?

_____

_____

_____

_____

3) When I said that "my request for deals was really a search for recognition," I had to pay attention to how I could get recognition through other, more fulfilling means. Can you write a list of ways you could get what you truly need, be it love, recognition, respect, etc…without the addictive behavior fix?

_____

_____

_____

_____

CHAPTER SIXTEEN

GOING WITHIN

Listen to your gut even when it leads you somewhere you don't want to go.

I know my Dad was sorry that my marriage to Clark broke up, although he said little about his feelings to me. In the same way, he said little about my relationship with Kurt. He was done criticizing me, and came full circle into accepting and appreciating me as I was. I'd forgiven and accepted him, too, just as he was. During the last few years of his life, we became good friends.

Dad fell ill in his late 70s, shortly after I married Kurt. Always passive, he would have done little about his health had I not taken him to and from the doctor, and advocated for him in the examining room. I asked lots of probing questions Dad never would have thought to ask. It wasn't just his passive personality—Dad came from a generation that does not think to question those in authority, like doctors. Since "authorities" meant little to me, I felt no such inhibition. Dad liked having me there and in fact, refused to go to the doctor unless I went with him. He knew I had his back.

I guess I could whine and ask why I always seem to lose people as soon as our relationship becomes good, but there is no point in whining. Maybe it's because healing is the point, and once that has been achieved, we are done.

Dad and I were riding a tide of good feelings toward each other when he died. He had gone into the hospital for surgery, but before the surgery could be performed, he had a major setback and ended up on life-support. The doctors cancelled the surgery, saying they believed there was no reason to do it anymore. They gave me the awful choice my father had to make for my mother—let machines prolong his life by a few weeks, though it could not give that life quality; or remove the life support and let him die quickly.

I did not want to make that decision. Not only because it's an impossible choice to make about someone you love, but also because my dad had told me he'd left his estate to me and my brother Jimmy, split equally between us. Dad wasn't super-rich, but he had done well, and I didn't want it to look like I had any money motives that my brother could seize on later to make trouble. I wanted him to share in the end-of-life decisions.

My brother. I haven't written much about him, and that's because he was no longer a part of my life, not even remotely. He was a selfish, screwed-up piece of work, a biker whose vision was narrowly focused on his own immediate desires. The last time we had even a trace of a relationship was when I was living with Duke—because Jimmy could always find drugs at our house. That was the only reason he came. In the years since then, I barely saw him. When we did see each other—rarely—we ignored each other.

But while our father was dying, I needed him. I couldn't make this choice by myself, and yet someone had to decide. I called Jimmy three or four times a day for three days straight, begging him to come and help make this impossible choice. I called, and called, and left messages and more messages. No response. Not one. Conference calls between Dad's doctors and the attorneys who drafted his Living Will—I had to do them alone.

Jimmy didn't show up until a couple of days after Dad died. He called me and said casually, "So what's going on?"

"Well, he's dead, Jimmy," I replied.

"Oh, okay," he said. "What are you going to do now?"

Maybe it was better that he didn't make a phony pretence of grief, but his total lack of concern stunned me anyway. I told him that after probate he and I would split Dad's estate. The next time I heard from him, he showed up at Dad's house with his biker buddies and a couple of trucks, and they emptied the house completely.

I let him take it. I wanted nothing to do with him and his cold and empty soul. I wrote him a check for half of the estate and that was the last time I saw him. My brother died shortly after my original draft of his book was completed. His estate held limited remaining assets. I can only wish him final peace—with himself and his choices.

My father's death, although a cause for grief, contained a huge gift. He left me some money, and since I took family leave from work to settle his estate, for the first time ever I had both leisure and time to ponder the deeper meanings in my life, rather than just react to events. I took advantage of grief counseling offered by my HMO, and there I met a most unique and interesting man who started me on the track that led directly to this book.

He was a Jewish doctor who practiced Buddhism, an unlikely combination on the surface, but his personality was so well-integrated that it gave me, a Christian, no pause at all. He had a striking method of speaking, using a calm and measured soft voice and pausing often between phrases as if he were listening to an inward guide. His kind brown eyes looked at me with compassion and not one ounce of judgment. I felt truly seen, truly heard.

My father's death dredged up all my earlier feelings around my mother's death, my adoption, and my issues with abandonment. My counselor suggested I use my time off wisely, that I allow my grief to unfold, and learn to embrace it. That sounded good to me, but "how" to do this was another matter.

He suggested that I spend time just being—learning to be still with myself so my inner voice could come forward. He said I had spent too much time being hard on myself, and had negated my ability to evolve to flourish.

Well, okay. The problem was although I could hear his words, for the life of me I didn't understand them.

Understanding would come in time, he said, and he recommended both journaling and meditation. Feeling adrift, but willing to trust him, I ambled through my days looking out the window at the trees beyond and thinking about being. When there was dead space, I resisted the impulse (and my habit) of filling it with things to do, things to say, even things to think.

Funny thing, no magic happened—at least not then, not when I thought it should. Nothing happened. Except that somehow I felt more peaceful, and I kept going back to see my Jewish Buddhist friend, and I kept journaling, and I kept meditating on being—even though I couldn't see it getting me anywhere.

I was learning to let go. I thought I should be learning to manage and grow relationships and other aspects of my life, according to my plans and goals. But really all this did was prevent God's goodness from coming in. When I let go, I allowed for something even better than my human plans to enter. The letting go slowly eliminated my toe-tapping impatience to make my life perfect.

Journaling helped to usher in this goodness, as I just followed my meandering path through meditating on being. At first, when I sat down to write, I had an idea of what I wanted to write about. Yet what I actually wrote often turned out to be very different from my original idea. Each day I woke up with a "great idea," yet when I sat down to write I had difficulty in making my pen communicate on paper what I knew. I would meditate or go into a prayerful process to penetrate the blockage. Each time I became stuck, the little devil on my shoulder said, "This is because you don't know what you're doing." I shrugged him off, some days more easily than others, and I tried to regain my commitment to my idea. But the paper usually remained blank.

I prayed and moved through the day with the intention to write although still unable to connect the dots and put my idea on paper. And finally, magic occurred. Whenever I've felt stuck in life, I've found that when I step out of the way of what I think I know, I make room for something greater to come in. In becoming vulnerable, I make room for inspiration. How strange and counter-intuitive to what we usually believe. I believed if I worked hard, applied myself, and stayed focused on my goals, I would profit. In deliberately moving into a place of not-knowing, of not-doing, I gained clarity. It's in the not-knowing where the real ideas emerge.

The words came, slowly. A few at a time, a sentence at a time, a paragraph at a time. As I followed them, something bigger emerged—I was creating my own learning through writing. Each revelation that unfolded on the page deepened my faith in the possibilities of good. And they deepened my understanding of the force in the universe making it all possible, a force I call God.

Reflections

It is so beautiful to realize that we are always where we're supposed to be.

Grieving my father, confronting the no-win choice of whether to keep him on life support; interacting with my dysfunctional brother—I would never wish for those experiences. But they widened my eyes and my heart, and as I moved through them, they gave me resources to heal my soul.

I can now understand pain, both mine and others. This understanding comes only from experience; there is no book or warning system that anyone can give us to teach us these lessons. Disappointment, a broken heart, or the loss of a dream can and will slam doors, but they open others. We recognize the lessons only when we accept them. With understanding, we evolve. Having God in your life helps because it gives us an anchor, knowing we are always where we are supposed to be. As we come to understand this, the pain we feel begins to diminish. What remains is love.

QUESTIONS:

1) When loss occurs are you able to receive it?

_____

_____

_____

_____

2) When difficult circumstances enter does your faith exit? Or is it challenged?

_____

_____

_____

_____

_____

_____

3) How do you restore your faith in difficult times?

_____

_____

_____

_____

_____

_____

CHAPTER SEVENTEEN

THE SPIRIT OF ALOHA

*Share your love with strangers as well as those
you consider safe.
In giving with no expectation of return,
love flows without effort.*

Sometimes you are growing and healing even when you think you are falling apart. We seldom see God's movement in our lives until afterward. Such is true of my sojourn in Hawaii.

Although I've attended various churches and read the Bible regularly, I don't endorse any particular religion. Since those gray, lonely days in Witness Protection, my basic spiritual practice has been prayer. Alone with God, we begin to tune in to who we truly are. However, once the stillness has given us some answers, I believe God wants us to share those gifts with the world. I have learned that I thrive best when I am in communion with others. I need others to mirror, reflect, and coach me in areas where I am stuck and cannot see the forest for the trees.

Hawaii drew me back to it again and again because of what Hawaiians call the "Aloha spirit." It's hard to define this to people who have not lived there, but it's kind of like that 1950s TV-fantasy world where the neighbors were just like family. People know each other, care for each other, do things for and with each other. If you live in Hawaii, all you have to do is be there, be one with the community, and the Aloha spirit will infuse your life.

As my law enforcement career wound down, I watched as coworkers only ten or so years older than me, retired and then died soon after. People can become so affixed to their titles, their performance, the regimens of their life, and their claims on power, that they forget what their lives are really about. When the dance is over and the music stops, they don't know what to do with themselves. I did not want this to happen to me.

After my dad left me a little bit of money, I felt I had an obligation to "pay it forward," not only to my kids, but to others, to myself, to my purpose here in the world. My purpose was not limited to going into holding cells. It was meaningful work, it paid the bills and brought me good benefits, but it was not the sum of who I was.

My inheritance brought me freedom, where before everything in life had been about "have to" and "must." Money gave me the opportunity to disconnect from those musts in order to answer the questions: Who are you? What drives you? What are you about? What do you dream? What do you want? How can I be of service to others? I needed to give myself permission to experience life and dreams. So I did, and set off on my own spiritual pilgrimage.

Hawaii was where I chose to begin. I didn't do it half-assed. I didn't just take a vacation—I moved there. My youngest child was in her last year of high school, and Clark and I worked it out that she would live with him for that year. My other kids were off on their own: Erica had graduated from UCLA, Tara from the University of Arizona, and Ryan would graduate the next year. The only one I took with me was Kurt, because at that time I still hoped a "fresh start" would help him—although he was not the reason I went.

This was the first time I took down time to serve myself. I didn't focus on my role as anyone's wife, mother, employee, servant, or E ticket ride. I spent time with myself, asking new questions. I no longer asked "How am I going to live?" Now I asked, "Who am I going to be in this life?"

In Hawaii I learned the value of just being. When you are being, instead of madly doing, you do not need to wear a mask. *Doing* isolates you and distracts you from being alone with yourself. *Being* encourages authentic relationships—even with strangers.

In the continental states it is called *small talk*, and is disparaged as trivial and meaningless. In the Islands it's referred to as talking story, and it's a valuable type of conversation. It means you are open to sharing experiences with another, that you embrace the community's ethos of sharing and encouraging, and experiencing random acts of kindness. Even strangers interact with an easy familiarity and respect. In contrast to the mainland, here people meet each others' eyes. People don't use Blackberries and iPods as electronic barriers to human interaction. The raw beauty of the Islands and their leisurely pace encourage human contact and simplicity.

I don't mean to imply that life in Hawaii was always easy. For one thing, I was still living with Kurt and struggling to understand why our relationship kept breaking down, no matter what I did. His ostensible plan was to start a new business, but, of course, he did nothing. From his perspective, my father's money meant he didn't have to work at all.

Our plan was to get spiritually healthy. We were going to read the entire Bible; I had always wanted to. I felt like a hypocrite when I claimed that Jesus and I were buds, but I had never read all of His words. Kurt went along with anything I said I wanted—he thought this kept me quiet and off his back, and since he never harnessed the discipline to actually read the Bible or do anything else he said he'd do, it allowed him to be free to pursue his other toys and interests.

The ironic thing was Kurt's do-nothing policy also set me free. It released me from caring about him one way or the other. I went to Hawaii to find my own center, and I didn't need him for that anyway. I followed through on reading the Bible, and I joined a Bible study group. The discipline of traditional Christian philosophy suited me. Highly mystical thinking is harder for me because the rules are too ephemeral. I have a need to know what is expected of me. I like having parameters because I need something to keep me accountable. Otherwise my impetuous blood can get stirred up, I veer off-course, and that's when I make stupid mistakes. Structure gives me ground to stand on. Until the day comes when I can define my own course by my own principles, I lean on the structure of Christianity because I know it comes from God.

Before I went to Hawaii, my relationship with God originated out of my own fellowship, heart and soul. I didn't attend church on a regular basis, and when I did, I didn't pay much attention to the sermons. I had no formal understanding of the faith, I couldn't recite any psalms or the Sermon on the Mount, and I didn't know how Christian principles applied to real life. In Hawaii, I studied all of these. This was my university on how to live life.

At the same time, I continued to pray, meditate, journal and use visualization exercises. I tried to have no goal or destination, but worked on becoming a blank slate so that my next step could find me, rather than me finding it. Previously, I had always set practical goals for my survival, like "Now I need a job," and "Now I need a house." But here I was in a place where I allowed for anything and everything.

Plenty of ideas came bouncing into my head during this process. I thought about going underground and working with girls from Russia who had been abducted for prostitution rings. I thought about teaching self-esteem to girls on the street, or girls in danger of going on the street. I thought about writing a book.

Whatever idea came into my mind, I journaled about it, prayed on it, and took it to my ohana for consultation and support. Ohana is a wonderful Hawaiian word that means family; more than family, ohana is your island, your community, whatever group of people you come together with. I had several ohanas in Hawaii. The incredible physical beauty of the Islands reinforced God's voice. I walked every morning, often as far as seven miles, along the beaches or through wild jungley parks, totally alone. Nature was my ohana, too.

It was on one of my daily walks on the beach that I met someone who was to have a significant spiritual impact on me. Her name was Robyn, and she was sitting on the beach with her husband as I walked by. In Hawaii, it is so easy to strike up conversations, because it is okay—indeed expected—to be aware of other people. When you are aware of someone, it is natural to acknowledge their presence. That is what I did with Robyn and her husband.

I sat with them for a few minutes, and then suggested we walk down the beach together. Taking a walk is a common way to get to know someone in Hawaii. Robyn's husband had to leave, but that first day, Robyn and I walked for miles. Our friendship took off from there, and we began meeting often, sometimes walking, sometimes talking, usually both.

Like me, Robyn had just relocated to Hawaii, and also like me, she's a small, fiery female. We are the same age, both petite, blond, with boisterous voices. She is remarkably open and unthreatened by the openness of anyone else. God, what a relief it was to not have to guard my tongue or censor my natural assertiveness, and know that I was not being judged, but accepted and valued just the way I was.

When Robyn speaks, you don't have to listen for agendas, assumptions, or hidden meanings. They simply do not exist in her conversation. It's so easy to trust her, to explore ideas with her because, although she has strong opinions, she does not push them on anyone else. She states them and invites you to accept them or not. She is not tethered to any outcome. In a conversation with Robyn, there's no right, no wrong, just free flowing expression.

Whatever I said, she did not react with commiseration, pity, or judgment. If I said I was not happy, she asked what I was I willing to change, rather than becoming the usual gal-pal co-conspirator confessing to similar feelings. She shifted the focus of responsibility where it belonged—on me. If I complained that a child was behaving badly, she'd fire back, "What does that mean to you? Are you open to shifting how you view this?"

Maybe the best word to describe Robyn's style of communication is compassionate probing. She probes for the heart of whatever issue is on the table. This is kind of humorous because Robyn's profession is a dental hygienist. She loves her job, and knows people are in her chair because she can help them see something that may not be working for them. For instance, if you came to her with dental problems, she wouldn't say, "Gee, it's too bad you're not taking proper care of your teeth." Instead she'll say, "Could it be that if you brushed your teeth more often this wouldn't be happening?" She's not pointing her finger and saying you're bad, or stupid, or wrong. She's just probing for an answer from you.

This is what she brings to friendship, too. When I shared something with her, she might ask something like, "Is this a common theme in your life?" And usually I'd have to admit it was. "Then it must have more to do with you than the other person," she'd say. "How can you change it? What are you willing to commit to?"

In Hawaii, I finally began to see the truth about my relationship with Kurt. Robyn had a lot to do with this, although she never said one word against him, or commiserated with me over his failures.

When I told her I was having nightly dreams about Gene, she asked me, "What does Gene mean to you now?"

"In the dreams he has Kurt's face, but I know it's Gene," I answered. She just smiled.

Later, I told her I was thinking about leaving Kurt, but I didn't know whether it was the right thing. He told me our relationship wasn't working because I wasn't really committed. So since his lease was due on his car, I took money out of my savings and purchased a lease for him to show my commitment.

"What do you think about me doing this?" I asked Robyn.

"You do what you have to do to find out what you need to find out," she said. "It can go either way."

Of course, during the divorce, I discovered Kurt took my name off the title—all part of his mission to squeeze as much out of me as he could before I'd had enough.

When I finally did decide to leave Kurt, I told Robyn that I now believed the marriage would never get better and it was finally over. "But Robyn," I added, "I'll be all alone."

She gave me a sympathetic look. "Honey," she said, "you've been alone through this whole relationship."

By holding up a mirror for me, without judgment, Robyn helped me understand that I was the cause and the answer to all things in my life, that my limitations were of my own making, as were my fears.

As this reality penetrated my awareness, I realized anew that I was also the agent for change in my circumstances and life condition. The reflection Robyn showed me spurred me to action.

Robyn taught me about integrity in relationships. Integrity means being whole, being who you are. So many of us—myself included—tend to lose our integrity when we're in a relationship. Robin taught me how to bond with another soul and still keep your own.

Meeting someone who is comfortable in their own skin encourages everyone's souls to emerge authentically, making true connection possible. Robyn's authenticity blessed my soul. Who she is never changed, and our relationship is not built on reactions to each other. It's built on mutual acceptance. It's no coincidence that I met Robyn in Hawaii. For me, she personifies the Aloha Spirit.

Reflections

Today, I can look into the eyes of a stranger and experience their soul. By leaving my own baggage at the curb and just being with that person, I come to them from a place of love. I don't invest in an outcome to our connection—we can simply be human with one another.

We can become so preoccupied with our own sense of self that starts to run our life, leaving many of us empty and alone. Our own advocacy doesn't allow much room for others.

Alone is something you feel when you withhold yourself from others. We have infinite self-imposed "reasons" for holding back—we are overextended, often self-medicated, we fear opening our hearts to someone new and being rejected. But this reticence isolates us, and that isolation limits our capacity for learning—and living.

I have found the greatest pleasure comes from being useful to a fellow human being, especially when it is least expected. It is in the giving that I receive knowledge about my own infirmities; it is through understanding that I move toward being a contributing member of the human race. And in loving, I am loved.

QUESTIONS:

1) How constantly do you keep promises to yourself? And others?

2) How willing are you to speak your truth in relationships?

3) In authentic living, transparency precedes credibility, followed by integrity. Journal about how this is represented in your life.

CHAPTER EIGHTEEN

DREAMS CAN COME TRUE— BUT NOT ALWAYS IN THE WAY YOU EXPECT

If someone betrays or disappoints you, forgive them.
They probably did the best they could under the circumstances—
you don't have to like itbut you must let it go.

———

I've had a lot of dreams. Some have come true, and some have not. Some dreams came true by my own hard work, and some by the grace of God. The dream I've had the longest came true because of both. And when it did, it didn't look exactly like I thought it would. Such is the nature of realized dreams.

As a child, I wondered, fantasized and dreamed about my biological mother, and even though I was never told anything, my dreams about her would not die. I secretly believed my "real" mother longed to know me, that she worried for my well-being. Another part of me didn't believe this was true—she gave me away, didn't she? The question "why?" tormented me for all my growing-up years.

It kept nagging me even after I finally met my biological mother. It took years—not because I couldn't find her, but because she was so cautious about meeting me.

After my adoptive mother gave me that first name, I tracked down the woman it belonged to, my half-sister's grandmother. She acted as the family's go-between, and I called her many times. It took several years before those calls bore fruit. My birth mother, Donna, eventually sent my sister to meet me first, so she could make sure I was not a lunatic or something worse.

My sister was excited about meeting me. She remembered when our mother was pregnant with me. She was the youngest in her family—the others were teenagers—so she had been looking forward to having a baby sister or brother. My newly found sister shared details of her childhood. It seemed that the older kids were often mean to her, and she resented her mother for making her stay with them so much. But when Donna came home from the hospital, with no baby, the family told my sister that the baby had died. When I contacted the family, the hidden secrets came tumbling out. It was hard for Donna to have to admit to lying, as well as to giving up one of her children, because it conflicted with how she saw herself. The truth didn't do my sister's relationship with our mother much good either.

I finally met Donna face to face when I was in my late twenties, shortly after I met Clark, and right after my other mother, who I now thought of as my "real" mother, died.

That first meeting with Donna was exciting and dramatic. The superficial similarities between us were stunning. I looked like her, for one thing, and she was beautifully turned out. Her clothes fit perfectly, no runs in her nylons, her lipstick matched her nail polish, her handbags matched her shoes. She had style, my kind of style. After my mother, with her muumuus and hair curlers, I was entranced. We hugged, and I could feel Donna's breasts, big and soft, just like mine. I sunk into her body and felt how much like my body it was. We went to her house, and the furniture, the carpets, the drapes, they all blended into a harmonious, comfortable whole. No magazines piled higgledy-piggledy in the corner. My God, it felt like finding a place I knew existed somewhere, the place where I belonged.

I was determined to not make Donna feel bad about giving me up, but to accept her on her terms. She told me a vague story about putting me up for adoption because she believed it was best for me, and although I doubted the story was as simple as that, I tried to go along with her "I did it for you" version. I wanted to show her I was simply thankful to have found her at last.

Shortly after our first meeting, we spent the day together and she invited me to stay over at her house. I was an adult with three kids of my own, but I was as excited as a ten-year-old at her first sleepover. During the day I tried to ignore the strained pauses between us, and her faintly critical remarks—maybe I was misinterpreting her, I thought. The next morning, I sat at her kitchen table, drinking a cup of coffee and watching her make breakfast for me. "I always wondered," I said idly, "what you thought about every May 13th."

She gave me a puzzled look. "What happened May 13th?"

May 13th is my birthday. Her response told me everything I needed to know—and not only about her. My whole dream about her missing me, wondering how I was doing, tracking my progress in her mind—that's all it was, a dream. I'd constructed that fantasy, and it had nothing to do with her at all. She gave me away, told herself that I was better off and then she was free to forget about me. So that's what she did. May 13th held no significance for her at all. It was just another day of the year.

As time went on, Donna and I both tried to develop a relationship, but it just never jelled. I experienced her as cold, critical, and cautious. She saw me as loud and demanding. Probably both of us were right. She picked at me for little things, and criticized me to my kids every so often. Every time she did, it felt like she rejected me all over again. I wanted her acceptance, I wanted her love, and I tried like hell to get it—which felt to her like I was demanding things she was not prepared to give.

Clark and I married shortly after Donna and I met, and I invited her to the wedding. She made snide comments about my gown, the decorations, and especially about the fact that we had a potluck wedding reception—how tacky! I was furious and said things I wish I hadn't. Who did she think she was, criticizing me after she threw me away? She had forfeited her right to criticize me.

One unqualified good thing came of meeting Donna—her parents, my grandparents. I had never had grandparents before; my adoptive parents might as well as come from chicken eggs as from people—they simply never talked about their families at all. My grandparents were so happy when I showed up, and they said all the right things: they had been against the adoption; they had wanted to take me instead; they felt like the prodigal child had returned; I was the lost child who had been found.

They just took me to their hearts right away, and they were such a warm and loving couple. It was the first time I'd seen a fully functional, long-term relationship between a man and a woman based on mutual respect. When my last child was born, I gave her my grandmother's name as her middle name. It made me very happy to claim our relationship that way.

I had my grandparents for about five years, until they died, within six months of one another. By that time, my sister and I bonded out of discontent with our mother—both of us looking for something from her that neither of us would ever get. Before we met, each of us thought the problem was us. It was affirming to know that the lack of mother-love wasn't my fault, or hers. It was simply not there. That was just the way she was—critical and guarded with her time, affection, and money.

In fact by that time I felt sorry for my sister and grateful that Donna gave me up, so I could be raised by a mother generous with her feelings, who taught me to be generous with mine. My sister can't get enough stuff to fill her emptiness because Donna was unable to give her time, attention or affirmation. Donna thought she was generous and spiritual—she studied with Deepak Chopra and Tony Robbins and was active in the new age community—but really it was largely on the surface. She could talk the talk all day with people she met in social clubs, but she couldn't walk the walk with people who were closest to her. She could discuss love on an intellectual level, but acting on it was different. She just wasn't comfortable with emotion.

After my divorce from Kurt, I wanted a new start, so I relocated to Southern California, which was where Donna lived. Our relationship had been sputtering along for over twenty years by then, and we still had not defined it well. Were we mother and daughter, female friends, or distant relatives who happened to share DNA? The definition of our relationship was less difficult than the dance we did within it. We established a tiresome pattern of getting together for an evening, irritating or disappointing each other, then breaking off contact for a couple of months, until we'd try again.

In my heart, I hoped that with the barrier of distance removed, Donna and I would finally connect on a soul level. Although she clearly needed little from anyone, including me, I desperately wanted to show her how good I could be at "being there" for her. I wanted to heal with her what I had healed with my father. I wanted her to recognize me as a decent, capable, and loving person. She was in her 70s by then, and I wanted her to know I would be there with her as she moved into the final stages of her life. If I am to be totally honest, there was a part of me saying: "See? This is how it feels to be loved, and I am able to do this for you—please let me share how it feels."

The soul-level connection I sought has not yet happened. I doubt if it ever will. Both of us must want it. Donna never wanted this from me, and I have nearly stopped trying. Our relationship is superficial now, because if we go deep it causes too much conflict. Yet I'm not very good at superficial relationships; they seem like a waste of valuable time.

Every now and then I get courageous enough to engage in another attempt to relate to her. Our last meeting was a date to see a movie together. I picked the movie W, which had just come out. It seemed safe because it was about politics, and politics was something Donna and I actually agreed on. We could see the movie and complain about George W. Bush for a couple of hours, and then go home and tell ourselves that we had connected.

We met for lunch before the movie, and she spent the entire meal complaining she didn't want to see W; she had enough of Bush in real life, why would I think a movie about him would be entertaining? Why couldn't I have picked something else? And why did I wear such low-cut blouses?

"Fine," I said, just to stop the flow of criticism. "Let's go see whatever other movie is playing at the same time."

"Fine," she sniffed.

When we got to the theater we found there was another movie starting just ten minutes later than W. It was *The Secret Life of Bees.*

I had never heard of the movie, nor the book by Sue Monk Kidd that it was based on. "What about this one?" I asked.

"Whatever you want," she said. I bought the tickets and since we had extra time, I suggested we sit outside on a bench and chat. She stomped over to a bench and sat down, and since she sat right in the middle of the bench I figured she didn't want me to sit beside her. I sat on a bench next to her, and she turned around and said, "Well if you're not going to sit on the same bench I might as well go in the theater." And off she walked.

I followed her, steaming. She gave me so much crap, every time I saw her, like she was trying to pay me back for daring to intrude on her life. Had it been anyone else, I would have told them where to go, but I can't with her, somehow. I spent all those years longing for her and here she is, and now I'm going to tell her to get lost?

So we went in to watch the freaking bee movie, which turned out to be about a girl whose mother left her and she's spent her whole life wondering why. Oh great. I sat rigid in my seat, trying to hold back the tears threatening to break through at any moment. My throat clogged, and my eyes stung. Donna was restless; she kept turning around and glaring at the people behind us anytime they opened a candy bar or shifted in their seat. By the second half of the movie, I gave up trying not to cry. I wasn't just dribbling from my eyes, I was boo-hooing into a wet handkerchief. By the time the movie ended I was hiccupping.

When we got outside the theater, Donna turned to me and said, "What's wrong with you?" like she really didn't know. Maybe she didn't—she was totally composed and dry-eyed. The movie that had so distressed me hadn't affected her one bit. She didn't connect it to our story at all, even though I sat right beside her.

"Nothing," I answered her. "I'm fine and I'm going home now." I left her outside the theater, and I haven't spent time with her since. That was last year.

Maybe Donna and I are done, and we'll never see each other again, but I'm keeping the possibilities open. I do know that I am done trying to make her be somebody she isn't. I'm also done trying to "win" the game we've been playing. Actually I'm the only one who has been playing.

If Donna calls me and asks for anything, I will be there for her, but I can no longer discount my own feelings and put myself out there for her to step on. I cannot force an emotional connection with her if she doesn't want it. Maybe she can't allow it. Maybe she criticizes me to keep me wrong, so she can be right. If she allows me to be a whole person then perhaps I would start to matter to her, and the feelings she suppressed might flower again.

How can I judge her for wanting to be right, and me wrong? Until the Bees movie, I don't think I fully understood I intended to show her she failed me by not being there. I wanted to show her how wrong she was and how right I was. This was a huge breakthrough in my understanding of myself. Perhaps we were both projecting a stance of righteousness. I believe in her way, she does love me, but it does not come across the way I want it delivered.

How I chose to see this was my choice. The irony is that criticism and an opinionated nature seems to be a genetic trait in our family. I can construct a wall that doesn't let her in or I can choose love and allow for our differences. When I am open to change and feedback I have shifted the potential for improvement for both of us and it becomes possible to change a self fulfilling prophecy (inherit in our family) of criique and commentary.

Reflections

No one ever said that once a dream comes true, you won't have to face adversity anymore. We're so focused on the joy we expect to feel once the dream is realized, we don't think about the challenges that might come with it.

It's up to us. You achieve an aspiration and find waiting for you, not a gold medal, a laurel wreath and bouquets of roses, but more hurdles stretching out into the distance. You can crumple, feeling you've become a victim of your own success. Or you can remember that each hurdle is a fresh opportunity for new, individual victories.

Instead of using our energy to hold back the inevitable, perhaps we should enter into discomfort with faith that a lesson is in the making. We can enter with trust.

When meeting my biological mother at long last didn't conform to my expectations, I resisted the truth, and spent a lot of time and energy trying to bend our relationship to my will. In short, I experienced frustration, but I also gained a sister and grandparents who loved me. My daughter bears the hallmark of that love in her name. Ultimately, I had to stop judging Donna's behavior because it didn't live up to my expectations, and when I did, it shifted how I viewed the experience of finding her. It is that new perspective on experience that I believe is a cornerstone of acceptance, which is a prerequisite for forgiveness.

QUESTIONS:

1) How and when did your expectations hinder a relationship?

___

2) Can you recall a time when you were open to an undesirable circumstance? For example, a challenging relationship with an employer, friend or loved one?

___

3) When you give up expectations do you experience a closer connection?

___

CHAPTER NINETEEN

GO BACK AND LEARN IT AGAIN

Courage through faith will get you where you need to be every time—even when you want to be elsewhere.

When I moved to Southern California in 2007, every day felt like the proverbial first day of the rest of my life. I suppose it actually was. For the first time since I was a teenager, I had no children's activities and schedules to maintain, no husband to care for, no demanding job to perform. My days were centered around only my own needs and desires. I was learning to be alone.

My God, it was scary. No structure except that which I created. Uncertainty over my abilities. Self-doubt about my willingness to persevere. Emptiness because I was not attached to anything familiar.

You would think I would have been prepared for this change. I'd sought it out deliberately, after all. But it turned out I based most of my own value on what I accomplished each day, and those were almost always tasks I performed for someone else. I could tally up those outcomes at the end of each day, and I sacrificed a true sense of my personal fulfillment for results I could measure. I grieved for my former life.

As the weeks turned into months, I grew more comfortable with my new reality. I did not concern myself with the day-to-day trivia of my loved one's lives; I didn't know what was happening with them unless they chose to share. It was time for me to decide what I needed. Now, I needed to conduct music for myself. In the quiet of the mornings and the long silences of the afternoons, I listened to the longings in my heart, and the voices in my head.

The voices spoke of pain, sorrow and disbelief. Pain for the suffering through the events that sacrificed my dignity and the years I spent plowing forward against all odds. Sorrow for the loves that I had lost, and the children who endured my ill-equipped efforts to parent them. Disbelief in where I found myself today—alone.

The longings of my heart told me it was time for a change in perspective and a new way of being. I needed to clear out the "stuff" which housed the beliefs and behaviors of the past. After the clearing, I could send out an invitation for something new to enter, something I would choose.

I acknowledged the truth about myself: without a partner I felt like there was a void in my life. Yet I know very well that, in relationships, I often lose myself. This is not intentional by me, or my partner. I wanted to learn how to be fully me, and still share who I am without being defined by the relationship.

In those long hours alone with the silence, I realized the value of a relationship where nobody is wrong, where both partners encourage flexibility and growth. I also spent a lot of time alone with my pain, but not wallowing in it—learning from it. I realized how much I needed a partner courageous enough to connect with his own pain and move past it. I cast those desires to the universe and trusted that God will bring me what is appropriate for me.

My job was to remain committed to this course, and not to become distracted by something different than what I requested.

So I practiced being by myself. For the first time, I went to a movie by myself, I dined in a restaurant alone. Initially, I felt like I should be doing something more, like something was missing. Soon, though, I stopped looking at this alone time as a waiting period, but as a season of dating—myself. Feelings surfaced that never appeared when my attention was directed toward someone else. I became aware how much I tailored my behavior to the moods, needs, wants or desires of others. Focusing on them allowed me to avoid myself and forego learning how to intelligently meet my own needs (without retail therapy).

I realized that previously I picked men who were unavailable—emotionally, physically, spiritually, or sometimes all three. They had little to contribute to a relationship. Yet, I thought I needed them. My fundamental need to be protected and cherished drove me to marriage, and it set me up for disaster. I was not protected and did not feel cherished in my childhood, creating a wound no relationship could heal. I had to create my own safety within myself, develop the ability to protect and cherish myself.

Eventually I felt strong enough within to move outward once more. I began that interesting process called "dating." I am a monogamous person who chooses committed relationships, so my experience with dating had been limited. I tended to cleave to one man, once someone who seemed viable appeared. Now that I was no longer driven to find a man to heal my wounds, I felt I could take my time. Again, I was unprepared for what I found.

The first thing I noticed about the men "out there" was regardless of his own age, physical attractiveness, occupation, income level or educational background, each man wanted a perfect love goddess: A woman without faults and blemishes, or at least a woman who keeps those faults and blemishes to herself.

The second thing I saw was that in the world of dating it's not who you are, it's who you want to be seen as. In his act, comedian Chris Rock says that in dating, everyone sends their representatives. He hit it right on. Although most single people say they want a real connection with someone else, few are willing to remove their costumes. Both men and women advertise their attributes as if they're walking down the runway of a fashion show, painting their self-portraits with amazing creativity and a super-sized dose of ego.

One of my first first-dates was with an attorney who clearly thought I should be flattered to be seen with him. He bragged about his divorce, how in the settlement he'd landed the multi-level beach house, which was perfect for romantic getaways in which he'd be delighted to share his body with me. But before the evening was over I learned that he was still legally married, although he didn't see this as a problem. "I'm an attorney," he said, "and I will know when the time is right—can't you see that?" I couldn't.

Another first date was with a wanna-be charmer who worked to be dazzling. At first, I admit, I was taken in. We shared a stimulating conversation, although his stories had clearly been well-rehearsed. The more closely I listened, the more I noticed those stories were all about him. His favorite activity was holding funfest weekends for his guy friends, where "boys can be boys." Quickly, his charm faded.

Then there was the hottie who relied heavily on his good looks because there wasn't much else to him. Communication was a strain. If I asked a question or started a conversation outside his practiced monologue, he looked blank. I probably looked frustrated.

After these encounters, and others like them, I drew up a list of traits I valued so I could try to avoid the time-wasters. Two top qualities I sought were leadership ability and consideration of others. I found a lot of men who believed they had these traits.

On one first date, Mr. X seemed to have these traits, and we set a follow-up date for dinner. But on the second date, Mr. X relaxed into who he really was. His idea of leadership was to order my dinner for me—without asking me what I wanted. I don't think he actually knows the definition of "considerate." After dinner, we parked along the ocean, where he promptly got out, instructing me to sit in the car and wait while he returned some phone calls. I handled it by doing the best thing you can do in situations like that—pop the top on a can of laugher.

And I've found many, many single men in my age group live in a special zone of their own creation: the Land of Me. They fill their lives with playtime hobbies—race cars, golf, boating, tennis, motorcycles, mountain biking, skiing, attending sporting events, playing in a band, etc, etc, etc. The Land of Me man reserves a sliver of his life for companionship, but only for occasional dalliances, and the woman who fills them must be willing to come and go at his whim. He's replaced relationships with hobbies, and is vigilant in preserving his self-designed status quo—a life with no interference. A relationship with a woman is a liability to these men. I got pretty good at spotting these men on first dates, and it was rare that I allowed them a second chance.

But I kept trying, honing my ability to recognize the types I had fallen for in the past, and this time walk away. Eventually I met someone who met the qualities on my list for real.

Funny thing, I didn't recognize him as a keeper at first. For one thing, he was a musician, and musicians often are so married to their art they have no room for anything else. For another, he didn't look like my type. As my daughter Tara said, "Mom, he's looks nothing like the guys you've been with. Usually you're with Mr. GQ or muscle guys." She was right. Val is cute, but he'll never appear in a Bow Flex commercial.

Val's parents named him after Prince Valiant, the hero of a long running series set in Arthurian England and featuring wild adventure and acts of chivalry. Pretty funny. Both his parents were teachers, but he was a rebel, foregoing formal education past Beverly Hills High School. Instead he became a rock musician in the 1970s and '80s, and he was still playing in a band. He loved the life.

Our relationship started sweetly by comparing our childhood war stories. This grew into sharing our values and opinions. Our conversations were long and rich. We had both learned to be honest about ourselves, so the getting-to-know you period was more transparent, not marred by the superficial dating dance. It wasn't long before our friendship based on mutual admiration for our differences and individual talents ripened into a love affair, and we began to grow an "us."

Even so, we both found it hard to let go of our distancing mechanisms. I was afraid to really be "us"—what if I made another mistake? My fear wasn't conscious—I was unaware of how I kept Val at a safe distance from "us" until my daughter Gina's girlfriend, Ashley, pointed it out to me. When I first met Ashley, I wasn't sure I approved of her relationship with Gina. Ashley is a "tell-it-like-it-is" kind of girl, a bit older than Gina, and I thought Gina needed more time to develop who she was on her own. For a long time I refused to call Ashley by her name because I didn't accept her relationship with Gina. If I had to refer to her, I called her "that girl." It amuses me now to realize that I never once asked myself what Ashley could be doing in my life. I now know that she was there to show me unconditional acceptance.

I developed the habit of calling Val my "little boyfriend," even though he's not short, or slight, or little in any way. I didn't say it in a mean way; I thought I was being humorous. But one night I gave a party and invited my family and all the new people I'd recently met. Many came from Val's musician community who I'd become familiar with, so the party was for them to jam together, as well as meet others in my world.

I did a lot of introducing that night, of this person to that one. As Val played music I would point him out to my friends and say "Hey, have you met my new little boyfriend?" If Val minded being called my little boyfriend, I didn't notice.

But Ashley did, and she called me on it. "You're doing to him what you used to do to me when you called me 'that girl,' " she told me. I saw immediately that she was right. When people get too close, I shooed them away by using some kind of protective mechanism. How blessed I felt right then to have Ashley in my life, someone who would tell me the truth without varnish, so I could hear it.

Everyone needs someone in their life who is not afraid to call them out. While we were together I stopped calling Val my little boyfriend. I started to call him my partner, and it suited our relationship much better.

Developing a relationship during the second half of life creates its own kind of challenges. You don't have kids to hold you together. You're not financially dependent on each other. You accomplished many significant "firsts"—first home, first child –before you met. You both have set your own parameters for how your life works. Plus you both have internalized some bad habits and boomerang behaviors. You may have constructed walls to intimacy over time, and those walls might be very thick by now. It's not easy to set new patterns in the second stage of life.

For Val and me, our previous patterns of blame/perfection and anger/resentment appeared like ghosts out of our past. We faced the same challenge—how to compromise and bend without losing ourselves in the process.

We chose to face this challenge together. Opportunities to practice popped up often. One of the things I've never been good at is impulse control. When something happens, I react immediately—and I previously responded strongly. I am learning to sit with my feelings for a bit before I say or do anything.

One Sunday, Val and I had planned a day together. That morning, before we got started on our day, I sat at the computer, writing, when Val came in and said he decided to do something else for a couple of hours. "You can stay here and write while I'm gone," he said.

My immediate emotional reaction was to want to say something along the lines of "Who do you think you are, telling me what I'm going to do?" Instead I said nothing, and just sat with the feeling for a minute, getting clear about why I felt the way I did. Then I said, "Wait a minute. I'm feeling that this is not okay."

He looked puzzled and said, "Why?"

"You assigned me something to do, but I didn't get to be a part of that decision."

He still looked confused. Val always set his own agenda, even within his previous relationships. In the past, I would have made this an issue. Instead I got up and said no more about it. I went to take a shower, and to think about how best to express my feelings.

When I got out of the shower I went up to him and smiled. "If you were playing a gig, and you wanted to do a solo on stage," I said, "wouldn't you talk to the other band members before you just broke out and did it?"

He laughed and said, "Point taken."

And that was that.

That was a minor incident. Perhaps I was afraid of someone trying to control me, and all the while I was actually controlled by my fears.

The fears remained, of course, for both Val and me. One of our greatest challenges was this book. As I was writing it, I shared it with Val. I knew I was taking a chance in doing so. Men do not always "get" women, and every man, even the "liberated" ones, want to feel a degree of ownership over the women they are involved with. Men want women's bodies and souls to belong exclusively to them. They want to feel that they're the only one who can fulfill their woman.

When Val read about the darkest moments in my past, he was shocked, dismayed, and confused. He asked the same questions everyone asks. "Why that? If you were destitute, or if you needed to rebel, why didn't you steal cars, or deal drugs? Why be a hooker?"

I tried to explain to him what it was like in my life then, that I actually saw beatings and abuse as a form of interest, and that once you are in that life, it's nearly impossible to get out—but he struggled to understand. I have remained committed to owning my name as a demonstration in accepting all the experiences in my life- good and bad without judgment or condemnation. In fact this was a big Ahah (even a mandate) when I was learning to love myself- full acceptance without self persecution.

Not all of his concern about the book is selfish. Much of it is because he felt protective and concerned for me. He asked me why I want to publish the book and thought I should keep it as a journal, if I have to write it at all. "Why give people the opportunity to judge you harshly?" he asked. "People are not always kind. They won't understand, and they're not going to be nice to you. All they may see is that you were a whore."

It's a good question. Why do I want to disclose my past to the world? Yes, in the past I've held back information I feared others would use to judge me—probably because I was still judging myself. After my pilgrimage to Maui, it became very clear that the value of my lessons lay in the potential for the encouragement they may offer for others. From then on, full disclosure was a soul mandate. When I fell for Val, I quickly—but not at all easily—put my cards on the table. I told him of my intention to develop a program for girls where the focus would be to provide tough love and encourage growth beyond limitation. Following the release of the book I would gain the support necessary to implement the Affinity Girls program. I shared with him that my story could serve as a platform and testimony that anyone's life can be improved through dedication, courage and correction.

Val remained unconvinced, but I no longer allowed myself to become trapped into a reactive conversation that went nowhere. I just responded, "You're entitled to your opinion and I'm sorry you feel that way." And I meant it. Val's process is his own. I can't change who he is, any more than I can change who I used to be. I do know that by exploring our pasts together, we nurtured a deep understanding for each other. Love flowed freely from that exploration, and it moved us to a new place, a place where he and I built a bridge that transitioned to a loving friendship.

What is so fabulous about my experience in this relationship was who I am now. We were two people from two different worlds and with two different belief systems each respecting the others view and individual journey. He kept his integrity while building that bridge—and so did I. When we parted we did so respectfully acknowledging we shared something special.

Reflections

Initiating an intimate relationship in the second phase of life is significant and profound. At fifty we are very different than the idyllic twenty-some things who first ventured into love without trepidation. We have loved, lost, risked, suffered, stumbled, and even fallen. We have scrapes and bumps and bruises. We have learned how to do for ourselves and survive using skills developed over at least thirty years.

In this new chapter, my wants are so different than they once were. Material acquisitions no longer fulfill me as they once did. I am no longer defined by the opinion of others. My profession does not summarize who I am. Family life is no longer at the center of my universe. The pursuit of personal happiness and peace of mind has become of greater importance. Who I want to be has conjured up dreams from my youth and I am inspired to let those dreams return.

My personal goal at the halfway point in my life was to develop a relationship with a man with whom I could celebrate life and coupleship. To me this means that both my partner and I remain true to ourselves while still being dedicated to each other.

I know now that well-meaning words and good intentions cannot alone create solidarity between two people. Solidarity comes when words and intentions are aligned. In the past, believed words plus action equaled integrity. It was a righteous position. I am learning how to be in relationship with compassion, rather than righteousness, and how to accept someone's differences without compromising myself.

So here I stand, naked, with my scars—both inside and out—shown clearly for my love to see. I am no longer hidden from the world. I have found the courage to share the truth of the experiences that once humiliated me. Can love truly conquer all?

Sometimes I am afraid that it cannot. But then I wake up and remember God's love is endless. It washes me clean and prepares me anew to share freely from its abundance. Here is where I find my best life.

QUESTIONS:

1) Has there been a situation in your life when people have loved you the wrong way (out of your comfort zone)?

_____

_____

_____

2) How did you deal with that?

_____

_____

_____

3) Did you feel compromised? Or as though your boundaries were being pushed?

_____

_____

_____

4) How did you handle that?

5) How does this differ from relationships where you honored your truth?

CHAPTER TWENTY

ALOHA, DEAR READER... AND THE BEST GOES ON

Love is the ability to extend yourself for the well-being of another.

This book has been about looking back at my life, and seeing my past as the necessary prelude to my future. I want to leave something of myself in the world, something that will make it a better place because I was in it.

My children are the best of what I had to give. Whatever I do with my life from here on, they and their children will constitute my most lasting contributions to the world. I tried to raise them to be independent, considerate and responsible. I think I succeeded. Or rather, they did.

I was a strict disciplinarian with my kids, probably because I knew what it was like to grow up without rules or structure. One day I overheard Val talking to Gina. Val is very laid-back, and he seems to think I was tough on my kids.

"Was your mom mean?" he asked Gina.

"No, she wasn't mean," she said. "She was strict."

"There's no difference," Val said.

"Sure there is," Gina corrected him. "We always knew what we could do and couldn't do. We always knew where we stood."

What a joy to know my children felt secure, because that is what I was trying to give them. I also pushed them to explore new situations and interact with all kinds of people. I wanted them to be able to handle whatever came their way. Listening to them talk today, I know I accomplished that too. They had experiences that many others didn't get.

Including having a mother who was just winging it most of the time. I learned how to be a parent while doing it. Maybe everyone does it this way, I don't know. But I'm pretty sure that in the beginning, at least, I was more clueless than most.

The truth is that my kids taught me just as much, maybe more, as I taught them.

Erica, my firstborn, has taught me grace and acceptance. She's always had an elevated awareness of people's souls, which is especially evident when she looks beneath the cruelty and bigotry she has experienced and sees the beautiful, fragile humanity we all share.

Erica endured the worst of my mistakes, and for a long time she was angry with me about them. That's okay—I agree I made some awful ones. She is very proper and sedate, in marked contrast to my outgoing personality. She calls me "Mother." If I curse, which I sometimes do (although I'm getting better), she'll say "Please don't speak like that, Mother." Erica's accomplishments are amazing, even when you don't know how tumultuous her early years were. A UCLA graduate, she's also a member of Mensa, the organization for people whose IQs are in the top two percent of the population. As a kid, she achieved everything from being elected Student Body President to acting in a Polaroid commercial and attending an actor's camp where Angelina Jolie was a fellow student. Essay contest awards speaking awards, and the Martin Luther King Sharing The Dream Award—she won them all. She even met Mother Theresa during an early voyage on Semester at Sea.

Several years ago, when Erica was a teenager, Gene died of a heart attack, and though she never knew her father, we went to his funeral together. It was less a celebration of his life than a survey of the wreckage he caused—hookers and ex-hookers, women he turned out and abused, and Erica's half-siblings, who he neglected. So many of them were drug addicts. And then there was Erica, with her quiet dignity and her capacity for forgiveness. What a miracle that such beauty could come from confusion and disturbance. Perhaps she represents some kind of redemption for Gene. It would be nice to think so.

My daughter Tara has taught me to persevere. Since she was only 16 months old when Ryan was born, she didn't get as much cuddling or special "Tara time" as I would have liked to give her. She and Ryan were babies together, and even then, she took on responsibility for him. The ideal big sister, I could always trust her to be sensible and strong, even when she was young. As a little girl, her favorite books were the "Little Miss" series—she is our own Little Miss Helpful. Her resourceful nature further developed as she grew into adulthood.

She birthed my first grandchild and adopted 3 children whom she has nurtured from humble beginnings to well adjusted youths. She has grown up to be the backbone of our family. When anyone is in trouble or has a problem, Tara is the first to stand up for them and the last to back down. When I was going through my divorce from Kurt, agitating and whining about how used I felt, Tara told me to "man up."

"You don't get to go down," she said. "This is your life, and your responsibility. You need to get over it. Now how can I help you strategize to get through this?"

Tara doesn't tell you what you want to hear, but she's great at telling you what you need to hear. She is our pillar of strength.

I regret for all of my children that they did not consistently have a father in their lives, but especially for my son Ryan. He deserved to have someone who could teach him how to be a man. He and Tara have met their father, Duke, and when he was a teenager, Ryan tried to establish a relationship with him. But Duke is still the thrill seeking, ego-centric person he always was. He's not capable of the selflessness required for fatherhood. Tara and Ryan wisely recognized this, and they have not tried to force him to make room in his life for them.

Ryan instead grew up surrounded by four dynamic females and a limited male presence, and it made him protective, loyal, supportive, and courageous.

He has no tolerance for behavior he considers immoral or unclean, such as greed or selfishness, and is an advocate for tough love, which can make him a little bit controlling at times. Yet, as an adult, he thanked me for setting such strict limits for him when he was a teenager, realizing that there may have been hell to pay if I hadn't—and he would have been the one paying.

His passionate morality doesn't make him judgmental, however. He's compassionate and understanding of people's faults, and he never jumps to conclusions. If anyone in our family has a problem and wants a measured, well-reasoned opinion, they turn to Ryan.

Ryan is all about working toward the greater good—for his family, for his community, for the world. Every day, he teaches me the value of simple decency.

My youngest child, Gina, at times felt overwhelmed by her three older siblings. When she was very young, I was learning how to juggle being a wife, a mother to four children and a full-time probation officer. I sometimes blew a fuse under all the pressure, until I learned how to multi-task. I deeply regret that two-year pity party I threw myself after Clark and I split up. Lost and brokenhearted, I spent way too much time whining about how I had to make it all alone. Her sisters and brother in college, her father gone, Gina was a pre-teen who needed my support, but I, too, withdrew. I remember many nights after dinner, I'd retreat to my room, and she'd go to hers. I could have spent that time with her, but I didn't. And you don't ever get that time back.

All this contributed to Gina growing into a cautious person, who is reticent to share too much with others. She is just learning how to comfortably find her voice and speak her truth. When she met her girlfriend Ashley, she separated from the family for a time, saying that she needed to learn "how to be me without you all telling me."

But she is also one of the most thoughtful people I know, guarding her words until she is sure of her position, weighing them carefully when she speaks. What a great lesson for me, who tends to shoot from the hip. Gina is loyal to those who share the gift of her love. And like her older sisters she is extremely competent in accomplishing any task she takes on.

I remember when I first discovered my grandparents, Donna's parents, and how thrilled I was to meet them. Connections are important—why didn't I give my kids more of them? They don't have any grandparents, aunts or uncles, cousins—at least none they truly know. They only have me, and each other. I hope that's enough.

Now my children are grown, and all four are fine people with hopeful futures. Their successes have come because of their own courage, tenacity, creativity, and the ability to handle whatever life has thrown at them.

Helping them grow up has been perhaps the greatest privilege of my life. But now that they are adults, and I'm no longer counseling people in jail cells, where do I go from here? As I write this, next month I will turn 52. I probably have at least twenty, maybe as many as thirty, years left to live. What contributions can I make during this time? What lessons have I learned in the last fifty years that might be helpful to others?

I hope that writing down these experiences, the agonies as well as the joys, helps others rise above their own pain. People keep calling me "unforgettable," and I hope it's because I've been able to bring them together with others, or prod them to change their lives for the better. When I've succeeded, it hasn't been because of me, but because the grace of God enabled me to shine a light on them.

This book is my attempt to shine a light for you. You are not stuck, no matter how deep in trouble you think you are.

We have all been broken. Every one of us. But your pain and adversity are gifts from God, powerful teachers showing you the path to wholeness. Our job is simply to heal ourselves, and in this process contribute something of value for others. It is here transformation begins.

Reflections

I'm still learning how to answer one of life's biggest challenges—how to honor the self in the face of whatever comes at you. Everyone answers this question in his or her own way. For me, I had to give my feelings permission to emerge, rather than squash them. For years, I didn't handle my emotions; they handled me.

When I was young, the hurt of being neglected and my feelings of powerlessness gave way to frustration then anger. I didn't deal with my anger, I let it run my life—experimenting with drugs, dropping out of school after the 7th grade, loitering on the streets of San Francisco, extended visits to Juvenile Hall. This path led me into the virtual slavery of my life with Gene, a relationship that made me feel even more powerless than I had before. It would be years before I could step up and assume full control of my life and responsibility for my choices.

I did it by acknowledging my feelings. I didn't do it deliberately, not at first. Without the isolation and quiet of life in the Witness Protection Program, I may not have have permitted that feeling of powerlessness to surface? In motion distraction is always available to keep us in denial of our true circumstances. Who knows how long it would have been before I called it what it was?

Once I fully acknowledged it, I took those first crucial steps toward acceptance and peace.

This alone did not address the scars of my past. After my father died, I realized I was now the matriarch for my family. I needed to choose and model mature, healthy behavior. I had to study my own emotional response patterns, and try to understand what was underneath them. First, I had to accept that my emotions were justified. Sounds obvious, right? I mean, it's natural to be angry when someone abandons you, or calls your daughter an ugly name. But for so long, I believed my survival depended on not acknowledging my feelings. I had to teach myself it was okay to feel.

That didn't mean it was okay for me to act on every feeling the second it bubbled up. I learned that when I felt something I wanted to avoid, it would ignite a burst of anger, and I would lash out with a barrage of unkind words that did not reflect my heart, but rather the scar tissue from of my past.

The trick was to feel the anger, but also to defuse it. Anger, of course, is a cover for other emotions I did not want to feel, like loss, sadness, fear, disappointment and betrayal. Defusing the anger was like unplugging a battery, the battery that sparked the anger. Without the battery churning up those sparks, I could see those other emotions.

As I began to allow just my feelings to emerge, to feel them without reacting, the spark occurred less and less. I tried to experience the emotions as they occurred, keeping them specific to the circumstance that prompted them. No more, no less. As I became comfortable with being uncomfortable, over time the emotions lost their bite. Lashing out became a distant memory, and "losing it" no longer a monthly event.

It means the breath of the divine is present. When you accept your sorrows and pain, you take the first step toward releasing them. When you say hello, you are also saying goodbye. Adversity is your friend. When it comes to you, embrace it, and say, "Aloha."

QUESTIONS:

1) Are you shackled to past should haves or could haves? If so are you willing to let them go?

2) Have you forgiven yourself for past poor choices? Do you believe people typically do the best they can with the information/skills they have at the time?

3) Do you allow others to hold you accountable for the past? If so what is keeping you attached to this as truth?

4) Are you committed towards living your best life while accepting past upsets?

_____

_____

_____

_____

5) Journal about how this looks to you, and begin a new dream of what is to come.

_____

_____

_____

_____

_____

_____

_____

_____

_____

_____

Blessings to you my friend.

Owen Valley High School
Library
622 W. St. Hwy 46
Spencer, IN 47460